# Struggle and Suffrage in Portsmouth

# Struggle and Suffrage in Portsmouth

**Women's Lives and the Fight for Equality**

Sarah Quail

PEN & SWORD
**HISTORY**
AN IMPRINT OF PEN & SWORD BOOKS LTD
YORKSHIRE – PHILADELPHIA

First published in Great Britain in 2018
by Pen & Sword HISTORY
An imprint of Pen & Sword Books Limited
Yorkshire – Philadelphia

ISBN 9781526712387

A CIP catalogue record for this book is available from the British Library.

Typeset in 11.5/13.5 point Times NR MT by SRJ Info Jnana System Pvt Ltd.

Printed and bound in England by TJ International, Padstow, PL28 8RW

Pen & Sword Books Limited incorporates the imprints of Atlas,
Archaeology, Aviation, Discovery, Family History, Fiction, History, Maritime,
Military, Military Classics, Politics, Select, Transport, True Crime, Air World,
Frontline Publishing, Leo Cooper, Remember When, Seaforth Publishing,
The Praetorian Press, Wharncliffe Local History, Wharncliffe Transport,
Wharncliffe True Crime and White Owl.

For a complete list of Pen & Sword titles please contact
PEN & SWORD BOOKS LIMITED
47 Church Street, Barnsley, South Yorkshire, S70 2AS, England
Email: enquiries@pen-and-sword.co.uk
**www.pen-and-sword.co.uk**

Or

PEN & SWORD BOOKS LIMITED
1950 Lawrence Rd, Havertown, PA 19083, USA
Email: Uspen-and-sword@casematepublishers.com
**www.penandswordbooks.com**

# Contents

This book is dedicated to the memory of
Norah O'Shea and local members of
the NUWSS and the WSPU who campaigned
for the vote on behalf of
the working women of Portsmouth
who 'did not have the time'.

# Preface

### ✳✳✳

What you put down on paper can often acquire a life of its own! I did not set out to write a political history. I fully intended to produce much more of a social and economic narrative but the constraints of time and space, and my own inclinations, produced this book which covers mainly the hundred year period between 1850 and 1950. I hope it does justice to a subject which has fascinated me since I discovered the campaigning Misses O'Shea when I was researching my *Portsmouth Paper,* 'Votes for Women', in the early 1980s.

The women's fight for the vote in Portsmouth was essentially a middle-class campaign: a campaign fought by middle-class women on behalf of their working-class sisters 'because they did not have the time to fight' as one suffragist put it succinctly shortly before the First World War. The campaign was driven by three main factors. Initially it was outrage that large numbers of women, needing to supplement what money they received from their soldier and sailor menfolk deployed overseas, or employed in the dockyard, were forced to work as sweated labour in local stay factories for pitiful sums of money. (The words stay and corset will be used synonymously depending on how the word has been used in the relevant source.) Younger women in turn supplemented what little they earned by working at night as prostitutes in the brothels and beer shops of the dockyard suburbs of the old town of Portsmouth, Portsea and Landport.

The introduction of the outrageously unfair Contagious Diseases Acts from 1864 played its part too. Interestingly their introduction did not provoke the reaction in Portsmouth which they did elsewhere. Possibly there was general acknowledgement in this particular town that the good health of the armed forces was of paramount importance. There were protests but equally many local prostitutes were very happy to be able to brandish a clean bill of health in front of possible patrons! However, the inconsistency in the treatment of the sexes inherent in the Acts not only drove resistance to the legislation and fuelled the campaign for their repeal around the country, but also spurred debate in the town as elsewhere on the general inequality of the sexes.

Thirdly, and of more concern to local women at the other end of the social scale, was the manifest lack of opportunities for unmarried, middle-class women who were barred by their sex from the professions. Working as a governess was one of the few careers open to them but as the Brontë sisters and Charlotte's heroine, Jane Eyre, discovered, the pay was poor and the women occupied an ambivalent social position. Portsmouth's satellite, middle-class, seaside suburb of Southsea had more than its fair share of such women.

In fact Southsea's elegant terraces and villas were described in the middle of the nineteenth century as a community positively dominated by women: young female servants and the women who outnumbered the men in their own families. These were the well-bred daughters of naval and military officers, active and retired, local business and professional men, and fundholders (individuals who lived on invested income). They remained at home until they married, and the restrictions placed on their lives meant that many never married.

This book traces the efforts of Portsmouth women to secure the vote in this 'most masculine' of cities, as it was described by HRH The Princess of Wales in 1992 when she was given the freedom of the city, and contemplated in her speech of acceptance quite why she had been given it! It is a story told within a general survey of Portsmouth women's lives, and their developing role in the life of the town from the mid-nineteenth century. (It became a city in 1926.) Inevitably this informed the efforts of campaigners to force the issue of equality both locally and nationally.

# Acknowledgements

\*\*\*

First of all, I must thank the members of staff of the Portsmouth History Centre who most courteously retrieved a very large number of records for me to study over a twelve-month period. Michael Gunton and John Stedman have also given me helpful advice about recent deposits of archive material which they thought I might usefully examine. Former colleagues, particularly Diana Gregg, helped me identify and pursue the suffragists, the Misses O'Shea, through the complications of the census records when we all worked in Museum Road. I am also grateful to Rachel Moriarty who lent me reference material on the Deaconess Community of St Andrew, and alerted me to the 'Song of the Shirt', and to Barbara Davis who told me about Mrs Haylett and her banner on Fratton Bridge. David Jordan gave me help identifying useful individuals for study.

I am also indebted to the many talented historians whose contributions to the *Portsmouth Papers* series, launched by Portsmouth City Council exactly fifty years ago in 1967, have created a wealth of information on the history of this city for use today. Such a resource is the envy of many much bigger communities. There are now almost eighty titles. Many of the writers have been local people but a number are working elsewhere, not only in this country but also in other parts of the English-speaking world. On my reckoning, this achievement represents at least 912,000 accessible, affordable words. It is new thinking on different aspects of Portsmouth's history – and each title is fully illustrated. I could not have pulled this book together in the time available to me without the help of many of these writers. So, thank you.

As for the illustrations in this book, they are, almost all, part of my own collection or from sources which are now out of copyright. For permission to reproduce the pictures of women working in Portsmouth Dockyard during the First World War, which were given to me some years ago, I am grateful to the Portsmouth Royal Dockyard Historical Trust, and for permission to quote from material in their care, I am grateful to the Portsmouth History Centre. Barbara Davis gave me permission to use Mrs Haylett's election literature.

Sarah Quail

## CHAPTER ONE

# Dockyard, Garrison and Naval Port

### ✳✳✳

By the mid-nineteenth century Portsmouth's population had more than doubled from 32,166 in 1801 to 72,096 in 1851, and would continue to grow significantly until the early twentieth century when it peaked in 1931 at 252,421. The growth of the town was chiefly the result of development of the dockyard although the ranks of dockyard workers, their wives and families were swollen by the soldiers and sailors who brought their families with them to Portsmouth. The population had in fact increased steadily from the late seventeenth century due to dockyard expansion. New housing spilled first onto the common fields and land outside the town gates. This development gathered momentum during the following century as new suburbs were built and continued steadily during the nineteenth and early twentieth centuries by which time almost all of Portsea Island had been built over.

Portsmouth is on an island site – Portsea Island – on England's south coast. The island measures roughly four miles by nine miles and is separated from the mainland by a narrow creek, Portscreek, and from the Isle of Wight by the Solent. The original settlement was established by a wealthy Norman merchant called John de Gisors c. 1180. It was situated in the south-west corner of Portsea Island at the mouth of the great natural harbour. A deep-water channel hugs the approaches along the island's southern shore. The rest of Portsea Island in the early medieval period was agricultural with scattered farmsteads and cottages, and several small hamlets and villages. There were two churches: St Thomas's Portsmouth, initially a chapel of ease to St Mary's, served the needs of the town residents, and St Mary's Portsea, in the village of Kingston in the middle of the island, served the more far-flung residents of the overarching parish of Portsea.

Richard I granted the town its first royal charter in 1194. Most importantly this meant that Portsmouth was now a borough with its own courts, independent of the administrative and legal reach of the county of Southampton, able to hold

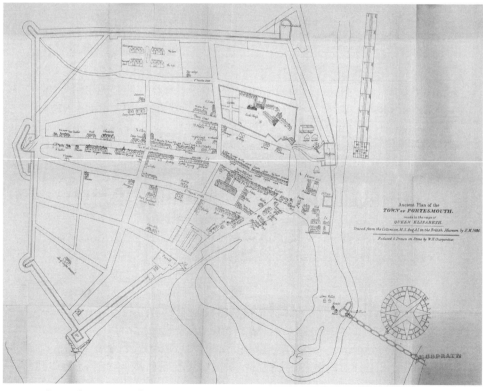

*Part of a nineteenth-century copy of an Elizabethan plan of the old town of Portsmouth showing St Thomas's Church, the Domus Dei and the area which became Point from Charpentier's* The New Portsmouth, Southsea, Anglesey and Hayling Island Guide, *Third Edition, 1841. Author's Collection.*

a fair annually for fifteen days and a weekly market. There was also widespread exemption from tolls. There was already a ship repair facility about half a mile from the town, to the north of an inlet of the sea known as the Mill Pond. There was also some sort of victualling depot, probably in the town itself, from at least this time if not before. The soldier-king quickly recognised the town's strategic importance as a link with his French territories and determined that it should remain under royal control and not fall into the hands of a merchant cartel capable of dictating terms to the king when he wished to use the port, as the town of Southampton was doing. Consequently during the thirteenth and fourteenth centuries Portsmouth was a rendezvous for expeditions to Normandy, Poitou and Gascony. By the early fifteenth century there was probably a ditch and wall round the northern, landward, perimeter of the town, and later in the century a stone tower, the Round Tower, was constructed on the seaward side of the town principally to protect the town and the harbour mouth from French raiders. Improvements were made to the fortifications over the next two centuries, culminating in a major reconstruction early in Charles II's reign

Henry VII designated the dockyard a Royal Dockyard and Portsmouth a Garrison Town in the early sixteenth century. With wars against the Dutch in the late seventeenth century, and against the French for much of the eighteenth century, Portsmouth was the departure point for almost every major expedition sailing from this country. The dockyard developed into a significant industrial enterprise as land was reclaimed steadily from the harbour for increased accommodation for ship building and repair, and the town itself spread to house the first waves of men and their families who came to work in the dockyard. Residential development spilled first, in the late seventeenth century, onto Portsmouth Point, the spit of land at the harbour mouth outside Point Gate in the old town. By 1729 when visitor Stephen Martin-Leake, a Clerk in the Navy Pay Office, described Point, there was 'one good street' and the area was 'populous' and thriving'. Point, he reported, was the 'Wapping of Portsmouth',

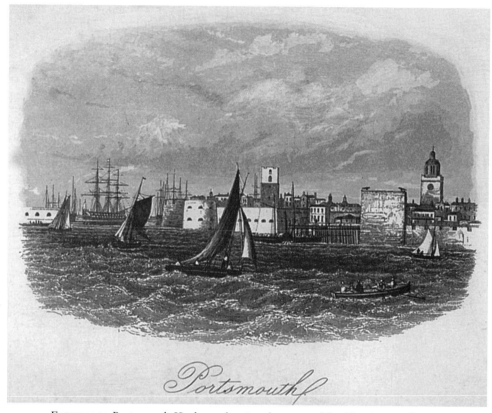

*Entrance to Portsmouth Harbour showing the seaward fortifications and, in the distance, the tower of St Thomas's Church from Lewis's* Illustrated Handbook of Portsmouth, *c.1860. Author's Collection.*

Here the Johns carouse, not being confined to hours, and spend their money for the good of the public, which makes alehouses and shops thrive mightily upon this spot. Some have compared it to the Point at Jamaica that was swallowed by an earthquake, and think, if that was Sodom this is Gomorrah; but it is by no means so bad as some would make it, though bad enough.

Shortly afterwards house building began outside the town walls on Portsmouth Common, common land to the north of the town and adjacent Mill Pond; and on the nearby East and West

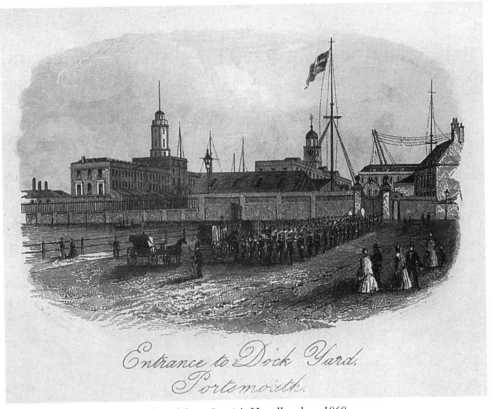

*Entrance to the Dockyard from Lewis's* Handbook, *c.1860.*
*Author's Collection.*

Dock Fields. This new development encircled the dockyard
from which it was separated by the dockyard wall. Confusingly
this area retained the name of Portsmouth Common for the
time being. The writer Daniel Defoe, visiting Portsmouth in
1724, said of the new development,

> Since the increase of business at this place, by the
> long continuance of the war, the confluence of people
> has been so great, and the town not admitting any
> enlargement for buildings, that a kind of suburb, or
> rather a new town has been built on the healthy ground
> adjoining to the town, which is so well built, and seems

to increase so fast, that in time it threatens to outdo for numbers of inhabitants, and beauty of buildings, even the town itself…

The new suburb rapidly developed a life of its own. By the middle of the century the shipwrights who lived there had raised sufficient money to build St George's Church as a chapel of ease to the parish church of St Mary's. A second church, St John's, also a chapel of ease, was built in 1787 to provide for the needs of the burgeoning population. The new suburb was fortified in the 1770s and under the Improvement Act of 1792 Portsmouth Common became the town of Portsea although it was never

*Lion Gateway, Portsea from Lewis's* Handbook, *c.1860. Author's Collection.*

incorporated. By the time of the first census in 1801 the local population far outstripped the residents of the old town of Portsmouth. There were 7,839 inhabitants in Portsmouth and 24,327 in the new town of Portsea.

The pressure on existing housing stock did not let up. Dockyard workers, soldiers and seamen continued to pour into Portsmouth during these years to build, repair and crew the ships which took the troops to fight revolutionary France. Further development began now. The working-class district known as Landport grew up to the east of the Portsea fortifications, again on former common fields. More significantly, and with serious implications for the future of both Portsmouth and Portsea, development began to the east of Portsmouth's walls, and Southsea's first smart terraces appeared between 1809 and 1812. Landport, Hampshire, King's, Jubilee and Bellevue Terraces faced the fortifications, and with cattle grazing on the glacis and rows of fine elms on the inner lines, these properties were marketed quite shamelessly to would-be tenants or purchasers as the properties of gentlefolk where it was possible 'to deceive the mind into the belief of its being a fine open park attached to the mansion of a nobleman'.

A promenade, later the King's Rooms, near the site of today's Clarence Pier, was constructed shortly afterwards. It was the beginning of Southsea as a fashionable watering place and the area developed rapidly. Local builders vied to lay out attractive streets and crescents and by the middle of the century the Borough Council, with the help of convict labour provided through the good offices of the Lieutenant Governor, Lord Frederick Fitzclarence, had drained and levelled Southsea Common. An esplanade was also under construction from the King's Rooms to Southsea Castle to better enable not only inhabitants but visitors to enjoy the sea air. It was sound investment on all sides. By this time most of the wealthier inhabitants of Portsmouth and Portsea had decamped to Southsea from the cramped and increasingly insalubrious walled towns where they were expected to keep inconvenient garrison hours. Visitors were rhapsodising too about the new watering place, 'the baths of every kind', called 'the King's Rooms', and Southsea Beach with its 'superiority over any other in the kingdom, for the clear sea-water, and the acknowledged utility which has followed the use of its baths in numerous complaints which bade defiance to medical skill'.

The consequences for both Portsmouth and Portsea of this shift of population to Southsea were serious. Many of the properties and gardens abandoned by their former residents were sub-divided into warrens of passages and alleys, and overcrowded dwellings. By 1850 Portsea particularly had become a foetid industrial slum. The ill-paved and unclean streets, woefully inadequate privy accommodation, and crowded courts with exposed middens and cess pits contributed significantly to the spread of disease and in particular the devastating outbreak of cholera in 1849. Walter Besant touches on the deteriorating quality of the area in his novel *By Celia's Arbour,* first published in 1878 but set several decades before then. His character Mrs Jeram was a tenant in a row of small houses known as Victory Row, off Nelson Street in Portsea, in the shadow of the dockyard wall. It was not a dirty or cramped court then, far from it. It was large and clean, and the adjacent dockyard wall itself was of warm, red brick with a broad sloping top on which wall flowers, long grasses and stonecrop grew. Overhanging the wall was a row of great elms, and a rookery. It all went though. The elms were cut down, and the wall flowers and grasses were torn from the walls. The court lost its charm and became squalid and mean.

Peace in 1815 had meant unemployment and poverty for many in the town. The irascible pamphleteer, writer and farmer William Cobbett might have been exaggerating when he wrote in 1823 that most of the houses constructed so hastily during the war years in Landport were now lying empty, but there was probably some element of truth in his writing. He described Landport as that great 'wen' (most towns and cities were described by Cobbett as boils or wens). Landport, he said, was stuck onto Portsea during the war,

No less than 50,000 people had been drawn together. They were now dispersing. The coagulated blood is

diluting and now flowing back through the veins. Whole
streets are deserted and the eyes knocked out by the boys
who remain... (one) gentleman told me that he had been
down to Portsea to sell half a street of houses, left him by
a relation and that nobody would give him anything for
them...

However, the advantages of screw propulsion over the paddle,
discovered in 1840, accelerated the move from sail to steam
and new trades of boilermaker, engineer, fitter and foundry
man took their place alongside traditional dockyard skills,
and by the middle of the century the workforce was back to
Napoleonic levels of nearly 4,000 men, growing to 5,000 by the
mid-1860s. The need for adequate space to accommodate the
new technologies combined with resurgent fears of war once
again with France prompted two further significant extensions
of the dockyard. A new steam basin was built on land reclaimed
from the sea in the 1840s and in the 1860s the Great Extension,
opened in 1876, trebled the area occupied by the dockyard from
99 to 261 acres which is essentially the space it still occupies
today. The population more than doubled now from 72,096 in
1851 to 190,281 by 1901.

Much of Portsea Island was still devoted to agriculture
when work on the dockyard extensions began but such was
the demand for, and pace of, house building that within fifty
years little farming land remained and many of the once fine
farmhouses had been either demolished or were derelict and
awaiting demolition for redevelopment, the value of building
land proving too tempting for their owners. Residential
development spread north and east along country lanes to link
by the early twentieth century with outlying parts of Portsea
Island: the former Domesday manors of Buckland, Copnor and
Fratton, and the hamlets and villages of more recent date such
as Stamshaw, Hilsea, Kingston, Milton and Eastney have given
their names to the neighbourhoods which exist today. Only two
remain of the elegant Georgian houses, 'seats of the resident
gentry' once living in these parts: Gatcombe House, c. 1780 and

*Detail from O.S. 6 inch Map showing the barrack complex in the north-east quarter of t on the glacis of the former fortifications) and, to the east of the Terraces, Owen's South.*

*; moving eastwards, the Terraces overlooking the Victoria Barracks (which were built
evised 1932. Author's Collection.*

Great Salterns House, c.1820. There are also a few old farm buildings surviving which belonged once to Middle Farm, Milton, and are now in Milton Park, and the outbuildings of Great Salterns Farm in Burrfields Road.

The new suburbs were not particularly attractive but they were respectable. Twentieth-century aerial photographs show close-built, gridiron street patterns, and terraced housing stretching away to infinity. Cyril Garbett, in due course Archbishop of York, and in 1918 Vicar of St Mary's Portsea, railed against the monotony of the streets in his parish,

> built without a spark of imagination. Row after row of red brick boxes, with square or oblong holes in their walls, while here and there a street glazed with hideous white brick, but you may walk through miles of our streets without finding a house which has any mark of beauty. Oh, the drab dreariness and ugliness of our Portsmouth streets!

He did not think much of the rest of the town either but while these houses might have offended Garbett's sensibilities they were palaces in comparison with the narrow streets and run-down accommodation of the old towns and the neighbouring district of Landport, and were the homes of a very particular breed of Portsmouth women and their children until well into the twentieth century. Perhaps these women were the descendants of those first waves of economic migrants from rural Hampshire and Sussex, many unemployed agricultural workers, who came to Portsmouth in the eighteenth and early nineteenth centuries to escape grinding poverty. They had to be tough then and were undoubtedly still tough and hard-working: the wives of seamen and soldiers deployed now to Portsmouth. There were no married quarters. Service wives lived in privately rented accommodation until very recently. When Garbett was writing, many of them were coming to terms with the devastating losses of the First World War. By this time, unlike their mothers and grandmothers before them, they may not have needed to work to supplement their husbands' pay but they still lived with the fact that one day news might come, as it did all too often, that the breadwinner had been killed in battle, or had gone down with his ship.

Portsmouth at the beginning of the twentieth century was still a heavily-defended naval port and garrison town despite the fact that the walls on the landward side of the old towns had been demolished in the 1870s and 1880s, redundant now due to improvements in the range and effectiveness of shore-based artillery. New barrack accommodation was built in their place for both the garrison itself and for the detachments of men passing through the town. By the early twentieth century there was an enormous military establishment in barracks in the north-east quarter of the old town of Portsmouth in Clarence, Cambridge and Victoria Barracks. Naval barracks were built at the top of Queen Street in Portsea between 1899 and 1903 on land previously occupied by the Portsea defences. Seamen had lived on board their ships in the harbour until this time but it was decided now to bring them ashore and accommodate them in barracks like the army. Other large-scale barrack accommodation included the Royal Artillery Barracks at Hilsea built in 1854 and the Royal Marine Artillery Division's buildings at Eastney, erected in the 1860s. By the outbreak of war in 1914 over twenty-five per cent of the town's male working population was in uniform (over 23,000 men).

It was impossible to ignore this formidable naval and military presence. The local population was accustomed to seeing men in uniform marching through its streets, from the railway station to barracks or ships, mustered on parade grounds, exercising on Southsea Common or lined up on Sunday mornings outside the Garrison Church. There were naval and military outfitters, chandlers and other suppliers of service essentials of all descriptions on the town's main shopping streets and thoroughfares: High Street in Portsmouth's old town, Queen Street and The Hard in Portsea, King's Road and Palmerston Road in Southsea, and Commercial Road and its adjacent streets in Landport. There were also hundreds of public houses.

*Royal Naval Barracks, Portsea, c.1906. Author's Collection.*

*Review on Southsea Common. The March Past, 1906. The Victoria Barracks are in the background. Author's Collection.*

They were located on almost every street corner particularly in the less affluent parts of the town. There were in fact almost 600 public houses on Portsea Island in 1914 owned by brewers Brickwoods, Portsmouth United Breweries and Longs.

As residential development spread inexorably north and east across Portsea Island and finally onto the mainland, the town's commercial centre also moved northwards from the old town of Portsmouth to Landport. A railway terminus was opened here in 1847 and discussions began as early as 1879 on the practicalities of moving the Town Hall to a new site here. The new building was opened finally by TRH the Prince and Princess of Wales, the future King Edward VII and Queen Alexandra in 1890. By 1904 the whole of Portsea Island had been incorporated into the borough and in 1920 the borough boundaries were extended further to take in the mainland districts of Cosham and Paulsgrove, once part of the parish of Wymering. They were extended finally in 1932 to include parts of the parishes of Portchester and Farlington. The borough was raised to the dignity of a city in 1926 and in 1927 the diocese of Portsmouth was carved out of the historic diocese of Winchester. A year later in 1928 the title of Lord Mayor was conferred on the new city's chief magistrate.

Portsmouth was badly damaged in the Second World War and large parts of the city, in particular the old towns of Portsmouth and Portsea, and Landport, encircling the dockyard, were devastated. Dockyard anti-aircraft fire saved the dockyard but German pilots, charged to destroy the naval base, emptied the arsenals in their aircraft holds over the neighbouring streets and their population. The war was a watershed. The relentless rise in the size of the local population was halted. Thousands left the city to fight, to escape the bombing or because their homes had been destroyed. Many never returned. By 1951 the population had fallen to 233,545. Forty years later in 1991 it had slumped to 177,142.

However, it can be argued that there was no real decline in the size of the local population. Many relocated to former villages north of Portsmouth, now part of what might be described as the unofficial greater conurbation. These families moved to

*The Town Hall, Portsmouth (not Southsea), c.1910. Author's Collection.*

Portchester, Widley, Horndean, Waterlooville, Bedhampton and Havant, all of which grew significantly after the war. Many were accommodated on the Leigh Park Estate in the borough of Havant. This estate was purchased by Portsmouth City Council in the dark days of the war quite deliberately, to house its displaced population in a new town of some 30,000 people. Interestingly the number of people living within the borough boundaries is on the rise once more. The population rose to 186,701 in 2001 and by 2011 had risen again to 205,100. At least ten per cent of the city's workforce is still employed in what is now called HM Naval Base Portsmouth, and the city's biggest industry is still defence although the shipbuilding, repair and maintenance element of the Naval Base was privatised in the late 1990s – early 2000s. Portsmouth is also the home port for at least two thirds of the Royal Navy's surface fleet.

Women move fleetingly through the early recorded history of Portsmouth. One of the earliest references to a woman connected with the town is in the tiny, probably late twelfth century, declaration of love of Jean de Gisors, Portsmouth's founder, for a young woman called Aeles de Lisle in a library in Paris: the *Bibliotheque National de la Ville de Paris*. It reads as follows,

> Jean de Gisors sends greeting to dameselle Aeles de Lisle, as to the woman he loves most in the world, although it is not his place (to have these feelings); and know in truth that he loves you as a man his sister; and that you can have the same trust in him as in one, or two, of your brothers … ; and know in truth that he would not wish to say or do any wrong towards you, any more than towards his mother.

It is not easy, over eight hundred years later, to be sure that this document is genuine but we do know from evidence in the cartularies of the Abbey Church of St-Martin de Pontoise which stood then outside Paris that Jean de Gisors had a wife called Alice who died in 1220.

There are references to women – sisters – nursing in the Domus Dei in the early thirteenth century. The Domus Dei, described in 1540 by the antiquarian, John Leland, as a 'fair Hospitale', was established by Peter de Rupibus, Bishop of Winchester c.1212. Its government was vested in a master, brethren and sisters who nursed and cooked for weary travellers and, in times of sickness, poorly local people. Their spiritual care was entrusted to priest chaplains. There is no more detail however on the sisters in either the foundation document or elsewhere. There are women's names, however, in early deeds of title calendared by Katharine Hanna in her *Portsmouth Record Series* volume, 'Deeds from Portsmouth and its area before 1547', published in 2008. The earliest deed, dated from internal evidence after 1133 and before 1144, cites a gift of lands from Baldwin of Portsea to the monks of Quarr for prayers to be said there for the souls of his father and mother. The lands however had formed part of his wife, Aeliz's, dowry. Other twelfth-century names in the deeds include Hysabel de Basevilla (after

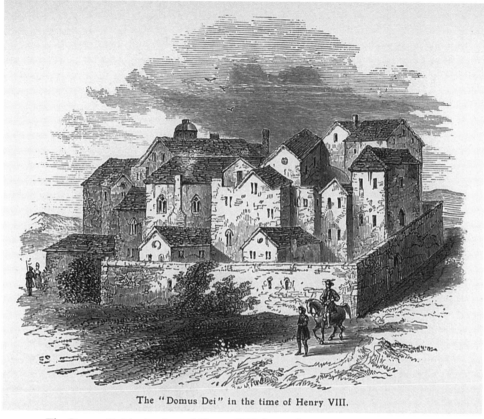

The "Domus Dei" in the time of Henry VIII.

*The Domus Dei in the time of Henry VIII from The Late Archdeacon Wright,*
The Story of the Domus Dei, *n.d. Author's Collection.*

1150 and before 1200) who is mentioned in the salvation clause
of a gift her husband made to Southwick Priory of an acre of
land. There is also Basilia, wife of Richard son of Daniel, who
features in a lengthy gift of lands which included property in
Paulsgrove. Ysabel de Wallop 'with the consent of Philip Morel,
her lord', made a gift of five acres from her dowry to Southwick
Priory, presumably as a 'sweetener' as she wished to be buried
in the priory church.

Wives such as Matildis wife of Girardus, Hadewisia de Port
and Adelidis de Port are named regularly in salvation clauses

at this time. Their subservient role – at least in legal parlance and practice – is underscored in the references to dowry wealth being used by their husbands, hopefully with the approval of their wives, for the men's own purposes. However, references to the need for women to defer to their lord's wishes or to act with the consent of their sons reflect not only women's subservience, but also the nature of feudal society. All people owed allegiance to the king and their immediate superior. In its essentials, this meant that the nobility held lands from the Crown in exchange for military service. Their tenants – vassals – in turn were granted the use of this land in return for homage and usually military service. Peasants who do feature in some of these early gifts lived on their lord's land, gave him homage and labour, and a stipulated share of the produce in exchange for military protection.

By the mid-thirteenth century there are references to women 'in independent widowhood' such as Edelina, widow of Galfridus Pelliparius, and Susanna, widow of William Russel. Later in the century, in 1289, there is Agnes de Merley who made a gift of her manor of Farlington to her son John, his wife Sibilla and their son, another John, 'in independent (*propria*) widowhood'. These are women who, for whatever reason, are holding land successfully, and have not remarried thus ensuring their independence. There is a marked reduction in the number of deeds – with names – surviving from the later medieval period. War and pestilence had taken their toll. The town was raided successfully by the French on four occasions in the fourteenth century in 1338, 1369, 1377 and 1380. By 1380 buildings were in ruins, and trade had been destroyed. The population had also been seriously depleted by the Black Death in the late 1340s. There are oblique references to women elsewhere however. It is clear from records of expenditure in Exchequer accounts in the National Archives that in the early medieval period Royal consorts and their servants stayed briefly in the King's House or Hall on their way to or from France.

Built by Richard I, the King's House stood on what is now part of Portsmouth Grammar School's present site in Old Portsmouth, as the area occupied by the original settlement is called today. In John's reign a chapel and separate quarters for the Queens of England were added to the complex. Individual women are cited too in surviving Borough Sessions papers from the mid-seventeenth century. They feature in a wide range of predictable cases in a town like Portsmouth: fornication, bastardy, abusing authority, illegal marriages, settlement, keeping a bawdy-house, theft, wife-beating, bigamy, rape, desertion and threats of murder. There are also women's names in registers of baptisms, marriages and burials of the two ancient parish churches: St Thomas's Portsmouth and St Mary's Portsea, again from the mid-seventeenth century. The registers do not survive before this time but there is no real detail in these records before the mid-eighteenth century.

During the sixteenth and seventeenth centuries several women gave substantial gifts of silver and silver-gilt to the town which to this day has the third best collection of civic plate in the country after London and Norwich. The silver-gilt Bodkin or Grace Cup as it was sometimes known was the gift of Mrs Grace Bodkin, the widow of Francis Bodkin who was three times mayor before he died in 1591. One of the outstanding pieces in the civic collection, it was made in 1525 and its shape and the Lombardic lettering hark back to an earlier gothic style. Mrs Bodkin also gave three parcel-gilt seal-top spoons of 1558 to the town, each picked on the seal with her husband's initials 'F.B.'.

Another widow, Mrs Elizabeth Ridge, gave a plain standing cup hallmarked 1619 and engraved with the words 'The gift of Elizabeth Ridge, widow, 1629'. The family's wealth derived from their brewing interests, and succeeding generations of the family made very large sums of money supplying beer to the navy. Mrs Ridge was clearly someone who was respected. There is an entry in the Election and Sessions Books for 1 March 1635/6 which notes that henceforth she should enjoy – most unusually – the freedom of a burgess of the town 'except the benefit of the common', i.e. grazing rights, 'in respect she had given a silver bole to the use of the towne'.

In another league altogether was the gift to the town of the Portsmouth Flagons, a pair of huge, silver-gilt flagons bearing the hallmark 1683. They were the gift of Charles II's French mistress, Louise de Querouaille, Duchess of Portsmouth, to the town (Portsmouth) from which she took her title, granted her by the king. She was also most likely a spy in the English court for her former master, the French king, Louis XIV. She was the mother of Charles Lennox, Duke of Richmond, by the king, and her descendants still live today at Goodwood House just outside Chichester. Louise never visited Portsmouth nor was she known for her acts of generosity. Why she made this substantial gift is a mystery.

Samuel Pepys's wife and female companions flit briefly through the pages of his diary when he is visiting Portsmouth, which he did on a number of occasions during his life. Their presence throws some light on the social mores and customs of the period. Pepys came to Portsmouth first on official business in May 1661 as Clerk of the Acts of the Navy, accompanied by his pretty wife, Elizabeth. He was captivated on the way down to Portsmouth by the wife of his clerk, Tom Hayter. She had worn a mask to protect her face from the sun and wind and he was keen to see what she actually looked like. She took the mask off when they arrived and he was pleased to note that she too was pretty. He had clearly been impressed by another woman, a Mrs Pierce, during this visit as on the journey home he and his wife 'did talk high', i.e. argue, 'she against and I for Mrs Pierce [that she was a beauty], till we were both angry'.

When he was in Portsmouth again, in April 1662, the town was full to overflowing with people and in a feverish state of excitement as the Portuguese Princess Catherine of Braganza was anticipated daily by ship from Lisbon to marry Charles II. Elizabeth stayed at home in London on this occasion and Pepys's work at the Pay in the dockyard took up much of his time but he did manage to contrive time to see the sights and enjoy himself. He saw the rooms 'all rarely furnished' which had been prepared for the princess in the Governor's House, and in chapel there he caught sight of Mrs Pierce once more. Seeing her passing by with another lady the next day he and his companion, Dr Clerke, invited the ladies to join them for wine and sweetmeats at their lodgings. The following day he abandoned his official duties and took the ladies sight-seeing. They saw the beautiful present which Portsmouth borough council had prepared for the new queen 'which is a salt cellar of silver, the walls crystal, with four eagles and four greyhounds standing up at the top to bear a dish' which Pepys reckoned was 'one of the neatest pieces of plate' that he ever saw. They then toured the dockyard and finally went back to the ladies' lodgings where they were joined by the doctor and played cards 'laughing very merry till 12 o'clock at night'.

In due course Pepys became Secretary of the Admiralty. He remained immensely loyal to Charles II's successor, his dictatorial and fiercely Catholic brother, James II, who had favoured Pepys and promoted him over many years. Pepys in fact did his best to ensure the navy could withstand William of Orange's landing in the West Country but his efforts were in vain. He resigned after James had fled to France and retreated to the then rural village of Clapham. In the meantime, strongly fortified and with an ill-disciplined garrison which had been doubled in size and was now easily the largest concentration of troops outside the capital, Portsmouth was caught up inextricably in the whole drama which played out in the chaotic November days of the 'Glorious' Revolution of 1688, and another Mrs Ridge found herself playing a role in events which she could not have anticipated.

She and her husband, Alderman Ridge, were descendants of Mrs Elizabeth Ridge and members of the same brewing dynasty. They were forced to give up their home in the High Street which was reckoned at the time to be the grandest house in the town to the infant Prince of Wales and his household. The child was the son of James II and his second wife, the Italian Mary of Modena. He was brought to Portsmouth where the fleet and garrison were still loyal to the king as a precaution, in case the royal family had to flee the country in the face of the invading forces of William of Orange and his English wife, Princess Mary. Mary was James's eldest daughter by his first marriage. She had been the Protestant heir to the throne until the recent birth of the Prince of Wales. William and Mary's troops had landed successfully in the West Country by this time and were marching now on London.

Such references to women are few and far between. The bulk of the references to women in the records before the mid-nineteenth century are mostly incidental. However, ironically, as a dockyard town, garrison and naval port, this town had large numbers of single women living and working here for much of its history: the widows, wives, girlfriends and 'common women' who came to Portsmouth with their menfolk and were then left, many of them, to fend for themselves while their men were away. As John Field points out in his PhD thesis, *Bourgeois Portsmouth,* the dimensions of female poverty were troubling. For most of the nineteenth century, dockyard pay was modest, the army made no provision for its men to send part of their pay home to wives and families while serving overseas, and the navy's scheme for seamen and marines was voluntary. Neither service made any provision for widows and children of men killed in battle during this period nor was it easy for women to earn a living wage when they had to care for small children. Had it not been for this large available female labour force, Portsmouth's corset industry would never have developed. By 1911 it was estimated that one fifth of Britain's stay makers lived and worked in Portsmouth. The preponderance of available female labour also meant that it was possible to drive down labour costs to pitiful levels which in turn drove women into prostitution.

## CHAPTER TWO

# 'Portsmouth Polls': Fact or Fiction?

### ✳✳✳

Portsmouth's prostitutes were legendary. After his ship had paid off, a skilful girl could inveigle Jack Tar's hard-earned money out of him in his first night ashore. Lively accounts survive of what it was like in the old town and its suburb of Portsea when ships were preparing to go to sea, or when they returned from lengthy deployments and famous victories. Thomas Rowlandson's iconic cartoon *Portsmouth Point* c.1800 captures such occasions admirably. Jack rolls drunk in the gutter, berated by his companion, her bosom spilling from her dress as the wine spills from the bottle she is clutching. A young seaman sweeps his female companion off her feet. Another man, an officer, tenderly embraces his elegant wife as his companions, her parents perhaps, his children and their nursemaid, gather round him. Another, we assume drunk, young woman is carried away while others sit on the laps of their sailor beaux. A one-legged fiddler is striking up a tune and a happy seaman with a girl on his arm is doing a jig of sorts.

William Walton's overture for orchestra, *Portsmouth Point,* depicted this scene in musical form in 1925, and in 1951 John Cranko choreographed *Pineapple Poll*, the Gilbert and Sullivan, and Rowlandson-inspired, comic ballet which is still in the repertoire of the Royal Ballet. It is good-humoured stuff but for contemporary diarists and letter writers, and local residents, the activities of Portsmouth's prostitutes were anything but

Portsmouth Point, *c.1800 by Thomas Rowlandson.*

amusing. The vehemence of their comments is disconcerting even today. Stephen Martin-Leake was not unduly censorious nor was John Wesley, the Anglican cleric and founder of Methodism who described the local population in 1753 as 'so civil a people I never saw before in any seaport town in England' but a few years later in 1758 General James Wolfe told a very different story. He described Portsmouth as 'diabolical'. 'It is a doubt to me', he told his mother, 'if there is such another collection of demons upon the whole earth. Vice, however, wears so ugly a garb that it disgusts rather than tempts.'

Writing in 1795, the splenetic Dr George Pinckard continued this theme. He did not mince his words. The streets, the houses, markets and traffic were not unlike that of other towns,

> but Portsmouth-point, Portsea-common, and some other parts of the town have peculiarities which seem

to sanction the celebrity the place has acquired. In some quarters Portsmouth is not only filthy, and crowded, but crowded with a class of low and abandoned beings, who seem to have declared open war against every habit of common decency and decorum ... The riotous, drunken, and immoral scenes of this place, perhaps, exceed all others. Commonly gross obscenity and intoxication preserve enough of diffidence to seek the concealment of night ... but here hordes of profligate females are seen reeling in drunkenness, or plying upon the streets in open day with a broad immodesty which puts the great orb of noon to the blush.

He describes in some detail 'these tender, languishing nymphs' with their Amazonian stature and crimson countenance, warlike features, brawny arms 'fit to encounter a Colossus', and their tattered apparel,

a loose flying cap, a man's black hat, a torn neckerchief, stone rings on her fingers, and a dirty white, or tawdry flowered gown, with short apron, and a pink petticoat.

Thus, he says, 'will you have something very like the figure of a "Portsmouth Poll"'. He was writing however on the eve of the departure of Sir Ralph Abercrombie's expedition to the West Indies when the town would have been crowded and in a feverish state of excitement, with rich pickings for enterprising locals, male and female. It is a similar story some twelve years later with war still in progress. An unnamed writer alludes again to the town of Portsmouth being,

low, and aguish; the streets uncleanly, and in many places wretched; but from the constant resort of seamen, a busy scene is presented. You meet companies of three or four sailors, each with his trull under his arm, whom he has decked out in flaring ribbons, and with whom he posts up and down the streets without any apparent object, from morning till night.

This writer refers too to the 'low alehouse' where 'Jack and a Portsmouth Parisot' can be seen in the vestibule dancing, 'to the elegant strains of two blind fiddlers'.

Happily, after 1815, few visiting diarists and letter writers are commenting on the perceived depravity of the local population. They remark more often on the novelty of the fortified citadel with its bastions, 'bristling with arms' and the presence of the fleet. The artist J.M.W. Turner was particularly fascinated by the fortifications on his visit in 1849 and he discusses the subject in great detail. The sketches he made on this trip survive in his sketch books in Tate Britain. The author of the pamphlet *Four Days at Portsmouth on the Eve of War*, Miss Bird, described the departure of the first division of the Baltic Fleet for the Crimea on 11 March 1854. She was staying in some style at the house 'fronting Spithead' of a high-ranking naval officer, possibly a property on Clarence Parade overlooking Southsea Common and Spithead. She captures admirably the drama of a fleet preparing to depart for war: the tension and the sorrow. She was moved particularly by two small boys,

> As we went down to dinner two naval cadets arrived; one looked about 14, the other about 12, little fair-haired boys to whom one felt inclined to say 'Does your mother know you're out?' Poor children, they might never know a mother's blessing again. I now realise the stern realities of war; the fictitious glitter with which I had invested it is gone.

She noted too the crowds at the dockyard gates and the hundreds of women,

> some clean and sorrowful-looking, others noisy and slatternly. All who could pay the enormous charges of the watermen were going or returning from Spithead; and at the stairs boats were thumping, women crying and boatmen cursing and swearing louder than all.

Their guide, a young Lieutenant, 'could scarcely elbow a retreat for us through the crowds of crying women, half-tipsy sailors, and grasping watermen clamorous to take us to Spithead'. There is no mention however of 'common women'.

Other visitors comment now on the new streets and squares developing to the east of the terraces in the new 'watering-place' and acknowledge the efforts of the borough council in delivering many of the recent improvements, particularly the drainage of Southsea Common. However, it is the sheer scale of the dockyard, thus far England's greatest industrial undertaking, which captures the imagination of the majority of writers. At a time when a Manchester cotton mill was employing a few hundred men and women, thousands of men worked in Portsmouth Dockyard. In fact only five firms in Manchester employed more than 1,000 workers in the 1840s and at the lowest point in the dockyard's fortunes, in the early 1830s, the workforce did not fall below 1,500 men.

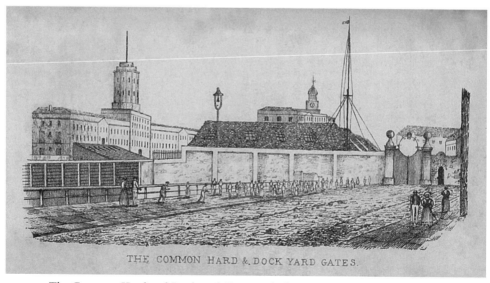

THE COMMON HARD & DOCK YARD GATES.

*The Common Hard and Dockyard Gates with the Semaphore Tower and store houses in the distance from Charpentier's* Guide, *Third Edition, 1841. Author's Collection.*

Visitors like George Simson, a tax surveyor from Hertford, described in meticulous detail his holiday in the Isle of Wight in 1839 which included a tour of the dockyard,

> the Mast Stores – Timber Stores – sawing machinery, making of the Blocks, saw one made throughout – pleased with the furnace for melting copper – drawing the iron out – the whole done by Steam Power – saw the Furnace at work for making anchors ... Went on board the *Queen*, man of war, the greatest ship in the Navy – will carry 120 guns – had been launched about 3 months – now in dock, many men at work on board, roved all over and under it.

The heat and drama of the anchor forges and the men who worked in this hellish environment, slaking their prodigious thirst with equally large quantities of beer, excited comment from most visitors.

But as John Field says in 'Bourgeois Portsmouth', the town, with its sailors, prostitutes and public houses had a reputation for immorality and what he calls 'irrational behaviour', which many will argue survives to this day. Improbable as it may seem, he records that it was suggested in 1824 that during the wars against France there had been up to 20,000 prostitutes in the town although many had now left. Local charitable endeavour was moved sufficiently however to set up the first Penitentiary Society in 1831 in Vincent Street, Landport 'for the purpose of reclaiming penitent women who have departed from the paths of virtue, and are desirous of being restored to respectable society'. By 1865, the year the first returns had to be made under the Contagious Diseases Act, there were said to be 1,335 'known common women'. Ten years later this figure was down to 494. Field suggests that before 1850 there was, on the whole, a general tolerance of Jack enjoying well-deserved rewards ashore – although local magistrates did not approve of girls being coerced into prostitution. Containing the problem in the poorer parts of the town and applying the law only when the women became public nuisances seems to have been local policy. Field quotes a local magistrate who pronounced that,

> If vice and immorality must exist – and they will, despite the law, at any rate let them revel in their obscurity, and apply the law only when they become public nuisances.

Attention began to be focused seriously however on local brothels – and the law applied – when in 1850 a full-scale riot took place involving several thousand soldiers, sailors and civilians in and around a White's Row brothel. There are reports now as well in Watch Committee minutes detailing prostitutes 'infesting' the streets and importuning men at night on Southsea Common, and reports of disgraceful scenes on Sunday mornings as soldiers were marched along the ramparts to services in the Garrison Church. There was another major riot, again in White's Row, in 1853 when a regiment had to be transferred to Gosport after its members rioted following a brothel fight. A few years later, in 1856, a hundred sailors wrecked a brothel in White's Row in revenge for an offence committed on one of their comrades.

Respectable local residents had had enough; 200 inhabitants of the streets adjoining The Hard complained in a memorial to the Borough Council in 1858 of the behaviour of drunken and disorderly soldiers, sailors, marines and prostitutes. Matters came to a head in 1860 when a dockyard boilermaker, Daniel Clewney, drinking in a Portsea beer shop, was murdered by militia men visiting prostitutes in the upstairs rooms. The Coroner's jury urged the authorities to suppress these 'dens of infamy' as did the *Hampshire Telegraph* and prosecutions began in more earnest. Two beer-shop keepers were charged with harbouring prostitutes and the police were ordered to be less tolerant and more diligent in bringing prosecutions. The prosecution of some seven licensees in February 1861 in fact prompted a public demonstration by prostitutes through the main streets.

The problem was essentially confined to the old town of Portsmouth, and to the adjacent suburbs of Portsea and

J. R. Pehning, Fine Art Dealer, 10 Elm Grove, Southsea.    a 211¦222

*The Garrison Church, c.1906. In the mid-late nineteenth century prostitutes would gather along the way or on the ramparts and scandalise respectable local residents by hurling abuse or shouting encouragement to the troops as they were marched to the Garrison Church from their barracks for Sunday worship. Author's Collection.*

Landport where men outnumbered women. Patricia Haskell calculated in *The Spirit of Portsmouth* that by 1861 Portsea's population had peaked at about 20,000 with males increasing since 1851 by almost 2,500 to 12,000, due mainly to more dockyard activity and a larger garrison in barracks. Females decreased to 7,967. She comments that with this imbalance and of course desperate poverty, prostitution was a natural consequence 'and notorious areas, some persisting well into the twentieth century, were Bonfire Corner, Blossom Alley, 'Yorke's Drift', White's Row and Rosemary Lane'. Haskell also highlighted the connection not only between beer houses and brothels, which was well-known to the authorities, but also between beer houses and lodging houses. Nearby houses in poor neighbourhoods were often rented to groups of girls, many of whom were employed in the poorly-paid clothing industry who supplemented their meagre pay by working at night as prostitutes.

Efforts began in the mid-nineteenth century to close down these lodging houses and continued well into the twentieth century. Legislation and municipal endeavour had some effect too. There were occasional prosecutions in local courts of notorious keepers of 'disorderly houses'. Then, eventually, prompted by the imprecations of successive Medical Officers of Health, most notably Dr Mearns Fraser who was Medical Officer of Health for 38 years between 1896 and 1934, some clearance of slum dwellings and their residents began. The Borough Council's first attempt at slum clearance in 1896 saw, among the buildings swept away, the demolition of Rosemary Lane but the cost of the venture deterred councillors. There is also evidence that a surprising number of the great and the good in Portsmouth were drawing rental incomes from slum tenements.

In 1975, one Portsea inhabitant told former police inspector and historian James Cramer that Miss Elizabeth Kelly, later Dame Elizabeth, owned 'courts' off Queen Street where local prostitutes lived. Based in the Town Hall, Miss Kelly ran Portsmouth's Relief Committee during the First World War and was made a CBE – Companion of the British Empire – afterwards for her war service. She was also appointed Portsmouth's first lady magistrate in 1920 and would play a key role coordinating the activities of local volunteers in the Second World War. Whether or not she owned courts off Queen Street, Miss Kelly would not have been alone among Portsmouth's better-off residents in having an income derived in part from the rents of slum properties. Surviving reports of inspections of dwelling houses in Portsea and Landport carried out in the late 1920s on behalf of the Borough Council's Health and Housing Committee give detail not only on the occupiers and the state of the properties inspected but also the owners' names and addresses and those of any agents employed. It is striking that the owners of most of the properties inspected live in the more salubrious parts of the town and a number live outside the borough in the leafy suburbs of Gosport, Fareham and other surrounding areas.

These slum properties constituted peoples' pension pots. Some owners looked after their properties and their tenants. Mr Humphries of 10, Grove Road North in Southsea was a case in point. He owned No. 2 Dorset Cottages which was in a narrow court, the entrance only 3ft wide, off Prince George Street in Portsea. Housing Inspectors described the property as 'kept in fair repair' considering its age, the owner personally carrying out repairs required. Two women, Mrs Franklin and Mrs Griffin lived there. However, more often than not, the verdicts on the houses inspected were damning: 'dilapidated', 'generally dilapidated', and 'very little money spent by owner on repairs'. Perhaps there were too many vested interests for it was not until 1910 that the first big slum clearance scheme was initiated with the clearance of Albion Street, Southampton Row, White's Row and King's Bench Alley, and their replacement with Curzon Howe Road, a tree-lined street of model artisans' dwellings.

The Contagious Diseases Act of 1864, prompted in considerable part by concern about the impact of venereal diseases on the health of the naval and military, initiated some reduction in the numbers of prostitutes in Portsmouth. The legislation empowered the police to arrest women suspected of being prostitutes in a number of ports and army towns including Portsmouth, subject them to compulsory checks for disease and, if they were infected, to confine them in a lock hospital or lock wards of a local hospital for treatment. The legislation was extremely controversial. The complete inconsistency in the handling of the sexes inherent in the Act played a key part not only in driving resistance to the legislation and the campaign for its repeal but also spurred debate on the general inequality of the sexes which was gathering momentum in the late nineteenth century.

There are lurid accounts in the Sessions Calendars of local women who had been confined, rioting in the lock wards of the Royal Portsmouth, Portsea and Gosport Hospital in Landport. On 6 July 1877 three young women: Ida St Clair (18), Maria

Leggett (20) and Julia Smith (19) were found guilty of smashing sixty-eight panes of glass in the windows of the lock wards. They each received six months imprisonment with hard labour. A few months later on 12 October 1877 another four: Isabella Wakeham (18), Lottie Treasure (18), Jessie Mayne (20) and Lilly Martell (19) were convicted of smashing forty panes of glass, twenty-two plates, thirteen mugs, a jug and a basin in the lock wards and were similarly punished. Few of them could read or write. However, by all accounts, despite the efforts of Portsmouth magistrates, local and central government, prostitution did not go away. In fact where some of the most notorious alleys and courts were cleared of their undesirable and unwanted residents those same residents simply moved into neighbouring streets.

However, the Contagious Diseases Acts can be associated with a steady decline in the numbers of prostitutes in the town. Child prostitution certainly declined very rapidly. There were thirty-one cases involving girls less than 16 in 1866 and by 1870 only thirteen such cases, and the girls were all over 14. Field notes that Mrs Colebrook of the Portsmouth Rescue Society, and Superintendent of the Protestant Home for Fallen Women, the original penitentiary, established in 1831, was adamant that the Acts drastically reduced the number of prostitutes in the town and interestingly there seems to have been little popular hostility to the Acts locally, despite national sentiment on the subject. There was only one 'indignation' meeting, in Landport in 1870, and in fact there was a petition from some local prostitutes for the Acts to continue in force according to the *Hampshire Telegraph* in March 1872.

Robert Dolling, the ritualist vicar of St Agatha's Church, Landport, more usually known by his parishioners as Father Dolling, understood well the connection between poverty and prostitution in his parish when he first went there in the 1880s. The streets were narrow and quaint, he wrote in his book, *Ten Years in a Portsmouth Slum*. Most were named after great admirals and sea-battles 'with old-world, red-tiled roofs, and interiors almost like the cabins of ships'. 'You could smell the sea', he said, 'a far-off scent coming over the mud of the harbour, and every now and then the boom of cannon, or the shrill shriek of the siren.' There were sailors everywhere,

> sometimes fighting, sometimes courting, nearly always laughing and good-humoured … I remember well how, the first night I made acquaintance with it, their uniforms and rolling gait redeemed from its squalor and commonplace this poor little district, with its eleven hundred houses and its fifty-two public houses. Charlotte Street was, from end to end, an open fair; cheap-jacks screaming; laughing crowds around them, never seeming to buy; women, straggling under the weight of a baby, trying to get the Sunday dinner a little cheaper because things had begun to get stale; great louts of lads standing at the corners – you can guess from their faces the kind of stories they are telling; then some piece of horse-play, necessitating a sudden rush through the crowd, many a cuff and many a blow, but hardly any ill-nature; slatternly women creeping out of some little public-house.

*Photo by]*  *[W. Barlier, Poplar.*

*Title page and frontispiece of Robert Dolling's* Ten Years in a Portsmouth Slum. *Published originally in 1892, this, the seventh edition, was published in 1896. Author's Collection.*

'Straggling under the weight of a baby', and 'trying to get the Sunday dinner a little cheaper'; 'slatternly creatures creeping out of some little public-house': these are evocative phrases which describe eloquently the lot of many of the women in this desperately poor parish. Dolling moved on to describe his 'district' further,

> Boys stole, because stealing seemed to them the only
> method of living; men were drunken because their
> stomachs were empty, and the public-house was the
> only cheerful place of entertainment, the only home of
> good fellowship and kindliness; girls sinned, because
> their mothers had sinned before them, oftentimes their
> grandmothers too, unconscious of any shame in it,
> regarding it as a necessary circumstance of life if they
> were to live at all.

There was nothing glamourous about these 'Portsmouth Polls'. They were driven to 'sin' by poverty, just as their grandmothers had been over a hundred years before. Only decent pay and housing would lift these women out of penury and its implications. However, altogether, they constituted only a small percentage of the total population and in fact W.G. Gates, on the staff of the newly-established local paper, the *Evening News,* from 1877, and editor of the paper from 1892 until 1926, took issue with Dolling and his picture of Portsmouth. Writing in 1928 in *Records of the Corporation 1835–1927* he maintained that by the end of the nineteenth century the moral improvement of the town in the previous twenty years had in fact been very great.

Other sources seem to bear him out. Diocesan Case Books for example survive from 1886 when a refuge was established in Somers Road by Winchester Diocese (the diocese of Portsmouth was established only in 1927). It was another place to go for help for girls and young women wanting to leave the streets. It is clear from the declining number of entries in the case books by the end of the nineteenth century and the beginning of the twentieth century that there was no longer such a demand for this sort of facility. It is also possible to plot in directories a similar decline in the number of institutions for homeless girls in Portsmouth before the outbreak of the First World War. There was more work available now for young women, and as the war ran its course women workers took the place of men in almost every local workplace, earning sufficient money to avoid the need to resort to the perils of prostitution.

The early case books are nevertheless a vivid record of what life was like for those at the bottom of the social scale. Each log sheet records the name and age of the girls, their residence before their 'fall', their last residence, religion, names of any friends who could be called upon, whether they had been admitted to hospital or needed to be sent, their behaviour and where they were sent to live while they learnt how to earn their livings. There is also a detailed paragraph about every girl's history. Poverty and abuse are usually the keynotes of each story. However, by 1886 there is at least a network in place equipped and able to support girls and women who wished to leave the streets.

Annie Lever was 17 in 1886. She went into service at 29, Nelson Street. Her behaviour was good. However, she 'walked out' in the evenings with a man with whom she 'kept company' and was seduced. She had a child of two months, no father, and a mother who was leading 'a bad life' in Aldershot. Alice Pearce was 18; her behaviour was good but she had been leading 'a bad life' in Portsmouth for some years and she was brought before the magistrates for stealing. The case was dismissed on condition that she went to a home. She promised Father Dolling that she would, and his sister, Miss Dolling, who kept house for him, brought Alice to the refuge and from there Alice was sent to a home at 14, Great College Street, Westminster.

Catherine Bates was 19 and was sent to St Thomas's Home in Basingstoke. She had been brought up at the Soldiers' Orphan Home in Devonport, had been on the streets in Portsmouth for only a short time and, after one of the Midnight Missions, went into Mrs Colebrook's Home. From there she was sent into service which she was obliged to leave because she was admitted to hospital. On her discharge she went to the refuge and asked to be sent to a home. Annie Saunders, who was 20, spent only a brief spell in the refuge; she was on her way to Canada thanks to Father Dolling. She had been two years in a home and having 'earned a good character', she and another girl were going to the St Margaret's Sisters in Montreal. She had no friends with whom she could stay while she prepared for the voyage, so Miss Dolling brought her to the refuge.

Sarah Clements was 25 and was sent to the Friendless Girls' Home in Bedwyn Street in Salisbury. She had been sent from London to a refuge in Ryde but was moved from Ryde to Portsmouth 'as they had some very difficult cases'. She had lived with a man for over a year, and had a child of 9 months 'for whom some ladies in London are paying for a time'. The man so ill-used her however that she left him. He threw a fork at her which put out one of her eyes. She was on the street for a time and then got a month in prison for drink. While there she had time to think 'and decided to try whether she would not be better off in a home' so she went to a refuge and asked to be sent away.

There are also startling histories of some very young referrals in the first volume of cases. The youngest must be Matilda James who was only 9 years old when she came into the refuge. According to the notes, she had been allowed to 'run wild' and play with boys. Her mother went out 'travelling about' and left the child in a neighbour's care. A young man 'ruined' her and she was brought to the refuge by one of the School Board Officers. She would be taken to live at the Deaconesses' Home at Fareham once she was well enough. Emma McFarlane was only 12. She was seduced by her uncle and a soldier, and would be taken to the Westminster home. Ada Wallace was 14. Her mother was 'a bad woman' and her father had gone abroad because of his wife's misconduct; Ada had been brought up by her uncle and aunt, both very respectable people. However, lately, she had become very troublesome and had been brought to the refuge.

Rose Huxford was 15. She had given her parents a great deal of trouble and run away from both home and her places several times. She was sent to a training home and then to a place at Bristol but would not stay long there. She had come back to Portsmouth and was 'about the streets' for a time. She then went to 'Mrs Colebrook's House', the Home for Fallen Women, but scaled the wall there in company with three other girls 'and went to one of the worst houses in Portsea'. There she clearly resolved to mend her ways and went to the Police Station with another girl and asked to be taken to the refuge. Two other girls listed, Bella Corrigan, 14, and Rose Gardener, 15, spent several days in brothels in White's Row 'but could not go on' with life there and made their way to the refuge.

The homes these girls were moved on to for their care, rehabilitation and training were legion. Collated from the first volume of case histories, they included not only 'Mrs Colebrook's House' in Portsmouth itself, but also several homes in different parts of London, and homes elsewhere, in Basingstoke, Salisbury, Brighton, Reading, Dublin and Wantage. They were funded by a combination of established and non-conformist church charities and private charitable donations. Besides this regional network, the support structure which existed locally also included the Portsea and Landport churches: St Agatha's in the heart of Landport and Holy Trinity, Portsea. Mrs Platt, the wife of the Vicar of Holy Trinity, Portsea, Thomas Platt, another ritualist, took girls to the different refuges herself as did Sister Dora and Sister Margaret, possibly from the Deaconesses' Home. Their names crop up on several occasions in the case histories accompanying girls to the refuge.

Directories provide a useful guide to the different 'caring' organisations, the scale of the different operations and some information on the motivated women who ran them. The 1889 *Kelly's Directory* lists a number. The Borough of Portsmouth Association for Nursing the Sick Poor was at 8, Gloucester Terrace, Southsea with Miss Day as superintendent. The Deaconesses' Home, with Head Deaconess, Sister Emma, was at 99–105, Victoria Road North. The Girls' Friendly Society Lodge was at 78, Marmion Road, Southsea and a similar institution, The Home for Girls, was at 18, Wyndcliffe Road, Southsea, both with their respective matrons. The Portsea Day Nursery, described more fully here as for 'the Care of Young Children while their Mothers are at work' was at 79, St George's Square with Mrs J. Allnutt as Manageress. The Portsmouth Rescue Society, and the Protestant Home for Fallen and Destitute Women, the longest-established of these different bodies was at 4, Brunswick Road, Southsea with

Mrs Colebrook, Superintendent, and Miss Jenkins, matron. The Diocesan Refuge whose case books describe so graphically the plight of the many girls and women who came through their doors, is described now as St Thomas's Refuge. It was still in Somers Road, Southsea and was clearly associated with the parish church. Miss Young was matron.

However, it is clear from these same directories that considerable rationalisation of provision took place in the years that followed, reflecting a changing need. By the end of the next decade, only the Portsmouth Rescue Society and the Protestant Home for Fallen and Destitute Women, and St Andrew's Home seem to be listed, with a single newcomer. The Portsmouth Rescue Society and the Home are in their new purpose-built premises at 4, Hyde Park Road with Mrs Colebrook still Superintendent and a new matron, Miss Ramsbury. St Andrew's Home is at the same address. The newcomer is the Southsea Ladies' Association for the Care of Friendless Girls at 2, Gloucester Terrace, Southsea, Sister Laura, Sister-in-Charge. One year into the war, in 1915, there are only two bodies listed. They are the Free Church Hostel Temporary Home for Girls, St Paul's House, 66, King Street, Portsea, Sister Florence in charge, and the Southsea Ladies' Association for the Care of Friendless Girls is now the St Thomas's Refuge for the Care of Friendless Girls at 2, Gloucester Terrace, Miss Staveley, Sister-in Charge. This presumably is the Diocesan Refuge, established originally in 1886.

By 1928 the local population had probably peaked at its pre-war level of a quarter of a million. Much of Portsea Island was built over and development had spread onto the adjacent mainland enveloping existing settlements south of Portsdown Hill in the hamlets and villages of Wymering, Cosham, Drayton and Farlington, and the borough boundaries had been extended in 1904, 1920 and 1932 to embrace this new housing. Local pride and patriotism was tested however when in 1923, as Editor of the *Evening News,* Gates would have published the news of the Blossom Alley Murder in Portsea which highlighted, as never before, the plight of those women still caught up in the vortex of poverty and squalid housing. The reports shocked not only local people, but the nation too.

On 26 January 1923 Mary Pelham, a known local prostitute, was discovered by a neighbour bludgeoned to death with a beer bottle in her tumble-down tenement in Blossom Alley in Portsea. She lived alone there with her cat. No one was ever charged with the offence although she had been seen arm-in-arm with a sailor earlier in the evening. What actually appalled readers of local and national newspapers which reported the murder was not the manner of her death but the circumstances in which she lived and died, and there was a public outcry. The room in which she was found measured barely 10ft by 5ft, and the height of the ceiling varied between almost 10ft and 7ft because of collapsing floors and ceilings.

The Liberal *Hampshire Telegraph* declared in a special feature on Portsmouth's slums a few weeks later that they were every bit as bad, if not worse, than London's,

> Portsmouth, as far as its slums were concerned, was comparable only with the big industrial towns of the North, where there was serious congestion and overcrowding in tumble-down and unhealthy houses, built in such close proximity that there was barely any air space ... How many are there in Portsmouth, apart from those compelled by force of circumstances to live their days in the squalid surroundings of our slums ... have the faintest conception of the deplorable state of affairs that exist?

Blossom Alley was described as 'a depressing passage, the opposite walls of which can be almost touched by extending the arms' and, with its nineteen houses and the five courts leading from it, was, said the author of the feature, like many similar, dreary and overcrowded lanes in the neighbourhood.

Mary Pelham was well-known in Portsea. Someone described her as 'a mother of the matelots'. Apparently she would hide men who were too drunk to make their own way back to their ships or to barracks. On the night she died she had been seen with a sailor heading home and was seen again some fifteen minutes later in Queen Street at the *Live and Let Live* where she said she was in a hurry as she had to get some chips for her 'chap'. Passing No. 14 Blossom Alley the following morning, her neighbour, Mary Riley, noticed that the front door was open. No one responded to her call. She went in and upstairs to the bedroom where she found Mary Pelham, the victim of a savage attack,

> the bedclothes were dark and in a sticky mass of blood. A gash from Mary Pelham's forehead to the top of her nose glistened in the light. Tied in a half-hitch around her neck was a light blue handkerchief or scarf. On the bed, the shattered parts of a pint oat malt stout bottle.

A sailor on board HMS *Ramillies* was taken in and questioned but was never arrested and formally charged with the crime, nor was his name ever released. Shocked, possibly by the adverse criticism, the Borough Council began finally to address the whole issue of slum clearance. They had built twenty-seven new houses in 1922 and 162 in 1923, the year Mary Pelham was murdered. The following year they built 221 houses, 421 in 1925, 682 in 1926 and 898 in 1927, and the following year, 1929, contracts were let to build small dwellings on a site at Hilsea and on the Eastern Road for the re-housing of tenants from Portsea dispossessed when their homes were condemned under the council's Slum Clearance Scheme. As Father Dolling euphemistically put it, girls 'sinned' as a necessary 'circumstance of life if they were to live at all'. With a sound roof over their heads and sufficient money in their pockets to provide some standard of living, prostitution ceased to be necessary.

## CHAPTER THREE

# The 'Song of the Shirt':
# Trades and Occupations

There were two key groups of working women in Portsmouth for much of the period between 1841 when the census first provides a detailed breakdown of women's trades and occupations and 1911, the last census before the First World War. The war proved to be a watershed and post-war census records demonstrate that local women workers had diversified into trades and occupations considered for much of the nineteenth century to be the exclusive preserve of men. The Second World War proved to be another watershed and this trend is amply confirmed in the 1951 census.

While the majority of women were, in the usual words of the census, 'without specified occupation or unoccupied', female domestic indoor servants, and the dress trades which included local stay makers were the two largest groups of occupied women in Portsmouth in the nineteenth and early twentieth centuries, and, as shown below, domestic indoor servants outnumbered the dress trades throughout this period, as they would have done elsewhere. The table also shows the correlation between the decline of what might be described as Portsmouth's two traditional female occupations and the rise of a female workforce in the late nineteenth and early twentieth centuries, which embraced a broader range of trades and occupations. The simple fact that residential servants had all but disappeared from most families' lives by the mid-twentieth century is an important fact in any consideration of women's lives generally in the late nineteenth and early twentieth centuries, but this is to get ahead of ourselves.

Servants were often a sore trial to their employers. Jane Austen knew about Portsmouth servants. She must have visited her distinguished sailor brother Francis, in due course Admiral of the Fleet Sir Francis Austen (1774–1865), when he

## FEMALE EMPLOYMENT IN PORTSMOUTH 1841 - 1951

|  | 1841 | 1901 | 1911 | 1931 | 1951 |
|---|---|---|---|---|---|
| **Total population** | 63,032 | 190,281 | 230,496 | 249,282 | 233,545 |
| **Total females** | 28,450 | 97,045 | 115,981 | 129,218 | 118,242 |
| **Occupied females** | 4,297 | 22,342 | 25,895 | 25,077 | 25,768 |
| % of total females | **15%** | **23%** | **22%** | **19%** | **22%** |
| **Indoor servants** | 1,977 | 9,354 | 7,788 | 6,042 | 1,209 |
| % of occupied females | **46%** | **42%** | **30%** | **24%** | **5%** |
| **Dress trades** * | 1,109 | 4,298 | 6,841 | 3,516 | 2,376 |
| % of occupied females | **26%** | **19%** | **26%** | **14%** | **9%** |
| **Other occupations** | 1,211 | 8,690 | 11,266 | 15,519 | 22,183 |
| % of occupied females | **28%** | **39%** | **44%** | **62%** | **86%** |

* For census purposes dress trades comprise dress and shirt makers, milliners, seamstresses, stay and corset makers; however, a separate figure for stay and corset makers was included as a footnote.

Stay and corset makers in Portsmouth 1841 - 1951

|  | 1841 | 1901 | 1911 | 1931 | 1951 |
|---|---|---|---|---|---|
| Total | 278 | 2,035 | 2,613 | 2,083 | 1,402 |
| % of occupied females | 6% | 9% | 10% | 8% | 5% |

Source: Census Records, Local History Centre, Portsmouth Central Library

was a young man at the Royal Naval Academy, Portsmouth and, no doubt, later when he was between ships. Jane's novel *Persuasion* was published in 1814. It features the large Price family who lived in glorious chaos and confusion in a very small house in the old town of Portsmouth. There the heroine, Fanny Price, newly returned from a lengthy sojourn with her Aunt Bertram, her mother's wealthy sister, at that family's seat in Northamptonshire, observes her own mother's 'trollopy-looking maid-servant' whose failure to stoke the fire or produce quickly the simplest of refreshments of tea, and plain bread and butter, depresses poor Fanny mightily.

When Mrs Price could finally give her mind to Fanny she could not resist inquiring about servants,

> A few inquiries began; but one of the earliest – How did her sister Bertram manage about her servants? Was she as much plagued as herself to get tolerable servants? – soon led her mind away from Northamptonshire, and fixed it on her own domestic grievances, and the shocking character of all the Portsmouth servants, of whom she believed her own two were the very worst.... The Bertrams were all forgotten in detailing the faults of Rebecca ... [the servant].

Further, complained Mrs Price to Fanny,

> Servants are come to such a pass, my dear, in Portsmouth, that it is quite a miracle if one keeps them more than half a year. I have no hope of ever being settled; and if I was to part with Rebecca, I should only get something worse. And yet I do not think I am a very difficult mistress to please; and I am sure the place is easy enough, for there is always a girl under her, and I often do half the work myself.

This fictional account is remarkably similar to the problems with her servants faced by Mrs Anne Knapp, the wife of the Reverend John Knapp, the Vicar of St John's Portsea. She wrote regularly to her eldest married daughter, Annie, who had married William Mayo, the son of another clergyman, the Rector of Folke, Dorset, in 1868. William was in the Royal Army Ordnance Corps and in 1872, the couple and their young family were posted to Bermuda. Mother and daughter wrote to each other for some three years until Annie and William returned to England. Problems with servants at the vicarage feature large in the letters. Mrs Knapp certainly had one servant, sometimes two, just like Mrs Price, and at least one servant lived in.

Jane Bird who was with Mrs Knapp for most of the time letters were exchanged probably lived out. She was a local girl and her mother was the vicarage family's washerwoman. Female laundry workers (washers and manglers), and charwomen, usually non-resident, were in fact 'locally important' in Portsmouth, as census documentation puts it, as they would have been in any urban area during the nineteenth and early twentieth centuries. Mrs Knapp wrote of Jane: 'little Bird is a first rate little body', but is 'too small to leave in charge of the house lest any strange person should come in our absence'. This was praise indeed, as was her opinion of Mary Hopkins who returned to the vicarage to work for Mrs Knapp following an absence to nurse her sick mother. Mary had 'become quite a good servant, so much improved'. More typical was Mrs Knapp's comment that she had 'a very dull sort of girl & cannot trust her to wash or do for Harold' (her last child who is poorly for much of the correspondence and died young). Mrs Knapp lamented further to Annie in a later letter: 'I have a most trying girl in the kitchen now, she tries poor Martin's patience sadly' (her second son, articled to a solicitor first in Portsmouth and then in London). Of another girl she wrote 'such a dirty muddle, so idle, careless and indifferent'.

Put simply it was very difficult to get good servants. When Mary left to live with an aunt, Mrs Knapp decided to see if she could manage with Jane alone for a time as there was, she wrote presciently, a dreadful set of possible servants looking for work, and they ask high wages as they are wanted at the factories and prefer its hours to service – every person who has servants is complaining and I fear these matters will get very much worse yet from various reasons, and we shall have to do the greater part of the work with some new 'domestic machinery' to lighten the actual labour.

Like Mrs Price, Mrs Knapp did a great deal of housework herself when her health allowed. She wrote one Saturday to Annie that she had been turning out and scrubbing carpets until she felt quite exhausted and longed for a rest on Sunday. It is possible that she was a difficult mistress but she was competing for staff not only with local stay factories, as she acknowledges above, but with more affluent households in Southsea. We must also remember that houses did get very grubby because of the smoke and fumes emitted by coal-burning fires and stoves, oil lamps and candles.

Ray Riley calculated in his *Portsmouth Paper*, 'The Houses and Inhabitants of Thomas Ellis Owen's Southsea', that at least a third of the 1861 population of Owen's Southsea was made up of female servants of whom at least two-thirds were between the ages of 16 and 30. The largest group of servants he identified in residence was at Crescent House in Queen's Crescent where Captain Henderson and his wife employed a housekeeper, lady's maid, housemaid, kitchen maid, butler, coachman and footman. At nearby St Vincent Lodge in Kent Road there was a cook, housemaid and lady's maid, and at Owen's own house, Dovercourt, also in Kent Road, there were four servants living in: a housemaid, cook, footman and page. In both instances these are surprisingly modest numbers of servants given the size of the two properties. However, it is more than likely that daily women – charwomen – came in to do 'rough' work such as scrubbing or possibly laundry, and the census returns do not necessarily reflect the true size of the domestic indoor servant complement in these houses.

According to Riley there were hardly any male servants. Of the women, almost all were single, and they lived in. Only four per cent are recorded as married. Most were recruited locally: in Portsmouth itself or in the neighbouring towns and villages of rural Hampshire and Sussex. A Register Office for servants was in fact set up in Queen Street as early as 1801. However, while Riley demonstrates, looking at birthplaces in the census records, that the majority of young servants in 1851 were recruited locally thereafter there is movement away from the area,

> almost three-quarters of servants aged 16 and under were born in Hampshire and Sussex, and ... there was a diminution down to the 31-40 age band as a result of new arrivals and departures of the locally born.

This must be due to the mobility of naval and military families. There is certainly evidence that servants in naval families, particularly nursemaids, moved with their employers – and charges – to Portsmouth.

It was not incumbent on employers to provide either married quarters or accommodation for their servants' children. This ruled out the employment of women with offspring whether married or widowed. Only childless widows were likely to secure employment. Single women with children found it virtually impossible, as a number of the histories in the Diocesan Refuge Case Books prove. Not only had these women offended the social mores of the period but unless their parents were prepared to undertake the task, they also needed to find someone able to look after their children. As noted already, there is in fact reference in one of the case histories to a young woman with a child who reported that a group of women in London had agreed to bear the costs of her child's upkeep 'for the time being'.

Women, as tailors, milliners, dress and shirt makers, seamstresses, and particularly as stay makers, played arguably a more significant role in the economic life of the town than those in domestic service accounting, according to Riley in his early *Portsmouth Paper*, 'The Industries of Portsmouth in the Nineteenth Century', for between twenty-one per cent and thirty-three per cent of the town's industrial employment between 1841 and 1901. They were not manufacturing naval or military uniforms. This was usually a male occupation. They were making not only traditional female apparel: hats, frocks, petticoats and outdoor clothing which was of course the lot of the trade across the country but also manufacturing shirts for the naval and military, and making stays, or corsets as they were more usually known towards the end of the century, initially for men as well as women. They undertook this work in their own homes and only later in the factories which sprang up in the town in the second half of the nineteenth century and petered out in the mid-late twentieth century. Stay-making was in fact as important in Portsmouth, 'localised' as Riley put it, as 'carpets in Kidderminster, straw hats in Luton, shoes in Northampton and cottons in the Lancashire towns'. By 1841 Riley suggests that the trade was already fourteen times more significant in Portsmouth than elsewhere in England and Wales and that it became in the course of the century the most important factory industry in Portsmouth.

There were good reasons why so many Portsmouth women worked in the different dress sectors. They were for the most part the wives of dockyard workers, the navy and military, and they desperately needed work for much of the nineteenth century. They also wanted work which they could do in their own homes thus enabling them at the same time to look after their families. Domestic service was not an option for women with children. Only later in the century would stay- or corset-making consolidate in local factories. These women needed work to bolster what sums their husbands earned in the dockyard where pay, certainly in the early years of the century, was lower than in nearby commercial yards. They also needed employment to safeguard against their men being put out of work with little or no notice. A workforce built up to meet a particular international situation could be stood down at the conclusion of hostilities or the end of an emergency with scant regard for the plight of the men and their families who still needed to eat and pay their rent.

Retrenchment, contraction, dismissals, and wage reductions for those lucky enough to be retained, was in fact the lot of dockyard workers for much of the century. At the end of the Napoleonic Wars in 1815 there were immediate discharges and by August 1816 it was reported by Henry and Julian Slight in their *Chronicles of Portsmouth* that there was serious distress with almost 600 people in the poor-house and 3,276 paupers receiving some sort of out-relief. Reduced activity in the dockyard after 1865 saw some 1,500 men summarily dismissed in 1868–9. There was little alternative employment available and in due course a fund was set up to pay for the emigration of the discharged dockyard men. The Admiralty made troop ships available and between 1869 and 1870 over 1,000 men and their families left for Canada where, according to Gates, most did well and prospered. Another thousand men, mainly shipwrights, were discharged from the dockyard in 1887 to the indignation and disgust of the town. It was the heaviest cull of the workforce since the discharges in 1868–9. The Admiralty maintained that redundant establishments had been maintained for too long by their predecessors and that reductions were now necessary.

Sailors' pay had seldom been sufficient to maintain a family. It had not been adequate in the late eighteenth century and it was still not enough a century later, as Father Dolling said when discussing the imprudent marriages which many ratings all too often entered into before a lengthy overseas deployment. Jack had scant regard for the financial consequences of his hastily-organised wedding,

> Marriages made like this ... do not always turn out happily, sometimes not well; especially as the man is often away three years at a time. For, after all, the half-pay is too often very little – seven and sixpence or ten shillings a week paid monthly, the first payment seldom being received before he has been away two months which means that the poor girl gets into frightful debt before she receives anything. I believe that in the Mercantile

Marine a woman can always get an advance note cashed. I trace back many grievous misunderstandings between husbands and wives, many children in semi-starvation, the first downward step in pawning, borrowing money at usurious rates, getting into such difficulties that only the most hateful remedy, which I dare not mention here, was possible, all to this difficulty of payment. Then, too, the sum, when received, is, if the woman has children, utterly inadequate.

The introduction of regular allotments of pay to wives mid-century was meant to mitigate these sorts of problems. Payment was made at the Dockyard Pay Office on production of a ticket but the system seems to have been discretionary in its early days. Allotments were often held up, sometimes between one commission and the next, and would continue to be a vexed issue until the outbreak of war in 1914.

Another reason why so many women had to work was to do with their sheer vulnerability when naval disasters occurred because, scandalously, there was no official provision for naval widows and their families. It was the custom for a public fund to be set up but there was little consistency in the sums raised which depended heavily, as today, on whether the appeal captured the public's imagination and roused sufficient sympathy. Further, the distribution of the sums raised was usually slow and inefficient. Finally, there were the needy wives of soldiers deployed abroad who wanted employment. Only a small number of soldiers, other ranks, were allowed to marry, usually some six per company, and married quarters were at a premium. Those who did marry without permission had to live out, and in his analysis of the mid-nineteenth century garrison in *Portsmouth Paper* 76, 'Old Portsmouth: A Garrison Town in the Mid-nineteenth Century', Riley has calculated that these men and their families numbered almost 500 individuals. Of these there were 138 wives and 145 children. Soldiers who lived out had to pay for their accommodation and support their families. As soldiers in barracks received free accommodation, food and clothing, the pay of those living out was modest in the extreme: some twelve shillings, half the pay of a dockyard worker. Such was the plight of these families that in 1854, at a special meeting of the Town Council, it was decided to urge the government of the propriety of making some provision for the wives and families of soldiers sent overseas.

However, such a preponderance of available labour created its own problems. Where there are more workers than jobs it is possible to keep wages low. This was an issue from an early date. A lively editorial in the *Hampshire Telegraph* on 14 January 1839 bemoaned the situation,

> An enormous quantity of these articles [shirts and stays] are made in the two parishes of Portsmouth and Portsea, to the manifest detriment of the poor-rates and the morals of the females employed, and which detriment and demoralisation arise from the infamous and unjustly low prices given for the work performed; the best workers cannot obtain two shillings a week, though they work early and late; and the fact will scarcely be credited that a dozen of seamen's shirts are made for ten-pence! and even this price has been known to be withheld on the alledgment that the work is bad; a better article called yacht shirts with full bosoms and stitched collars and cuffs, are made at 2*s*. and 4*d*. per dozen. At these prices the wretched females cannot earn more than 2*d*. a day.

'Sweated' labour, as it was called, remained an issue throughout the century. Thomas Hood's poem, 'The Song of the Shirt', published anonymously in the Christmas edition of *Punch* in 1843 might just as well have been composed with the plight of Portsmouth's shirt makers in mind. It was composed in honour of a Mrs Biddell of whom little is known other than the fact that she was a very poor widow and seamstress who sewed shirts and trousers in her home using the materials given her by her employer. Desperate to feed her children, she pawned what clothing she had made. Too poor to redeem the pawned items, she finished up in the workhouse. Her story became a byword for the wretched conditions in which she and so many women like her worked, and a catalyst for those trying to improve the lot of such women. The first stanza of the poem was a powerful rallying call,

> With fingers weary and worn'
> With eyelids heavy and red,
> A woman sat in unwomanly rags,
> Plying her needle and thread –
> Stitch! Stitch! Stitch!
> In poverty, hunger, and dirt,
> And still with a voice of dolorous pitch
> She sang 'The Song of the Shirt!

Portsmouth was described at a meeting of the Tailors' Union in a local hall in December 1913 as 'the worst sweated town in the three kingdoms'. The speaker, Mr Rowlerson, the London organiser of the union, stressed this point further,

> His Union had determined to spend some money and energy in Portsmouth in the New Year. They were anxious to avoid trouble of any kind, but the condition of affairs in the tailoring trade in Portsmouth must cease. Girls of 16 and 17 years of age worked from 8 a.m. to 8 p.m. for sums ranging from 1s. 6d. per week upwards. If our English officers knew of some of the conditions their uniforms were made under he very much questioned whether they would ever wear them. The Trades Board Act in the tailoring trade gave a minimum wage of 13s. 6d. for girls over 18 for ordinary work. Yes girls employed in Portsmouth on some of the very best work were receiving less than half the sum laid down by the Trades Board Act. His Union meant to put up a fight to improve the conditions of the workers in Portsmouth.

Initially women, like Mrs Biddell, had worked in their own homes so little investment was required. A likely entrepreneur could set up a simple depot which supplied the women with the requisite materials which they then made up as stipulated, by hand, and returned to the depot. Advertisements in the local newspapers provide clear evidence of this 'putting-out' system. One published in the *Hampshire Telegraph and Sussex Chronicle* on 18 July 1846 sought 600 female white shirt makers and stay-stitchers and gorers who could be sure of employment if they applied 'at the Factory, Union Road, Landport'. It was not actually a factory with sewing machinery in the sense of a Lancashire cotton mill or a Yorkshire woollen mill. It was simply a warehouse for storage at this stage. There is also evidence in directories that several London firms had a number of stay warehouses in Landport, attracted doubtless by the prospect of cheap labour.

By 1911 there were 2,613 stay makers and the industry which was what it had become by now was firmly established on a factory basis. The factories were not large in spite of their importance nationally. One of the pioneers of mass production locally was William Helby who lived at St Margaret's in Yarborough Road in Owen's Southsea. He, his wife and son established one of the earliest factories in the town in Kent Street, Portsea. Leethem Reynolds began in a small way in Canal Walk in 1844. The Canal Walk premises were expanded in due course and branches were established in All Saints Road and Common Street. The All Saints site seems to have been the largest stay factory in the town with a rateable value of £260 by 1885. By then however, seven stay factories had rateable values over and above £100, and Chilcot and Williams had a rateable value of £87. The trade flourished in the late nineteenth century. New firms were established such as Charles Bayer whose Regent Street establishment, with a rateable value of £289 in 1901, was second largest to Leethem Reynold's All Saints Road site with a rateable value of £369. Other new names included Royle and Co., and William Fletcher whose factory stood in Landport Street and in 1901 was the third largest in the town. Fletcher began as a factory manager and then set up on his own but financial mismanagement led to bankruptcy in 1904 and he was bought out by Leethem.

Personal accounts of what life was like in the stay factories are almost non-existent much before the early twentieth century. We know from what material does exist: a limited range of secondary sources and some original documents such as local newspaper reports, the criminal Sessions Court records and the Diocesan Case Books, that for much of the nineteenth century stay manufacturing was sweated labour. The women were exploited, and paid very little. There are references to girls resorting to prostitution to make ends meet. The only business records of a stay manufactory surviving in the City Records Office are those of Chilcot and Williams. A James William Chilcot is listed in a Post Office Directory as a stay maker in Surrey Street, Landport in 1847. He entered into a partnership with Thomas Roger Williams in 1869 and the firm retained this name until the factory, still in Surrey Street, closed finally in 1970. It had been taken over by Berlei (UK) Ltd in 1965 after the last Williams to be associated with the firm died in 1962. Partnership agreements, minute books, reports of annual general meetings, lists of shareholders, correspondence, account books and stock-keeping records, all survive, but there is no personal information in the collection about the women who made the stays and other garments with which the firm was associated. You have to look elsewhere for this sort of information.

Leethem (Twilfit) Ltd's eldest pensioner, Mrs Le Santo, aged about 95, was interviewed for an article which appeared in the *Port of Portsmouth Chamber of Commerce Journal* c.1950. Despite her age she was 'erect and dignified',

> her well-shaped head crowned with wispy white hair. We talked: She had worked at stays since she was twenty and was pensioned at eighty-three. Fifty-six years of that time with Charles Leethem & Co. and Leethems (Twilfit) Limited, of whose present Chairman she

spoke with admiration and affection, and of his mother 'that perfect lady'. She had loved her work, especially managing the girls in her charge. No, her husband was not French; his people were all Devon stock. Her first job had been in Spring Street, but she could not recall the firm's name. That would appear to be the first of the Portsmouth corset-makers. Then she went to Canal Walk and later to Sultan Road. On the anniversary of her first birthday after leaving (she was eighty-four) she was invited to Sultan Road factory to celebrate. A ten-pound box of chocolates and a great bouquet fittingly crowned a happy day. 'Good girls they always were and would always do all I asked! Yes, I've always had good health' brought up six children – a pain in the back lately, but I haven't been to a doctor. I've ordered my funeral though, so there'll be no fuss. He asked me if I would pay a deposit. I said no, I might fall overboard and drown and the money would be wasted!

Photographs survive from c.1918 of women working in the machine rooms at Weingarten's factory. The women sit at their machines in serried ranks wearing aprons to protect their clothes, in some cases wearing their hats too. Very similar photographs survive of later generations of women, sitting, still with their aprons on but without their hats, at work stations in Leethems (Twilfit) factory in the 1930s and 1970s, and in Chilcot and Williams' own factory in the 1950s. Their recollections of factory life between the end of the First World War and the late twentieth century have been recorded, however, in a remarkable series of oral history interviews conducted c.2000 jointly by Portsmouth Museums and Records Service, the University of Portsmouth and Portsmouth Royal Dockyard Historical Trust with financial support from the Heritage Lottery Fund. Edited highlights were published in a booklet in 2002, *Fingers to the bone. Recollections of corset workers in Portsmouth* and it is here – and in the recordings themselves – that we learn something of what life was like for the actual workers.

After the First World War, conditions improved for those working in the dress trades. To start with there were no longer the same numbers of women seeking work as there had been before the war as the care of soldiers' and sailors' wives and families had improved, as had wage rates generally. Many of the women recorded for the oral history project were delighted to secure work in one or other of the local firms. News of vacancies was passed on by word of mouth or secured through family connections, and girls started work straight from school aged 14 after the First World War, or 15 after the Second World War. Before 1918 they may well have been as young as 11, and before 1880, 10 years old. There seems to have been plenty of work between the wars as well as in the years immediately following the Second World War. One woman explained that there were not too many alternatives then to the local dress factories. Both Commercial Road in the city centre and Palmerston Road, Southsea's premier shopping street, had been destroyed by enemy bombing and there was no shop work to speak of.

You learned in the stay factories on the job, initially under the tutelage of an older employee, often sprinting with messages across the factory floor or even between the different factories belonging to your firm which were likely to be spread across the town. One young machinist spoke of having to walk – tram fares were never offered – from Eastney in the south-east of Portsea Island to Landport in the centre of town and then on to Sultan Road in Stamshaw, and back, in the course of a day, a journey of at least six miles if not more. After a six-week unofficial apprenticeship you were expected to know enough to begin earning your living. According to Hilda Preston, a machinist and supervisor between 1947 and 1981, you would be placed 'in more or less a team, or a bench. There were long benches and girls were sitting opposite each other at one stage, and then they changed it and you all sat behind each other.' There might be two or three hundred girls working in a factory according to a male corset worker employed in the mid-twentieth century, and the noise of the sewing machines could be overwhelming if you were not used to it. The girls where he worked made bras and corselettes and he believed they were well paid. They may well have been. Gwynneth Daly, a stitcher and seamer between 1947 and 1955 recalled that office work was poorly paid at this time and if you wanted 'to earn the money, into the corset factory you went... .' When she married her husband in 1955, she was earning £10 in the corset factory, and he was earning £7 in the dockyard. 'Yes', she said, 'that was the difference. Of course, the harder you worked in the corset factory, the more money you got.'

A girl who began work at Leethems in 1920 said that most of the factory was working then on servants' dresses which were made up in black, grey or brown poplin. The firm also made linen kitchen aprons with bibs, 'ladies chemises and French-style knickers, all white'. However, most of the interviewees talk of their work making corsets, the older women describing long corsets made of 'heavy', stiff material with rows of hooks. Leethems' white chemises were unusual. Most of those recorded speak of pink and peach-coloured materials with very little white. Even when nylon 'step-in' corsets were introduced after the Second World War they were still in pink or 'tea rose'. The women talk in some detail about the technical aspects of their work and also about working conditions.

Management was strict. You had to be on time in the mornings and clock in. If you were more than three minutes late, you lost a morning's pay. Most women worked from 8.00 a.m. until 12 noon and in the afternoons from 1.30 p.m. until 6.00 p.m. There was Saturday working from 8.00 a.m. until noon and, 'if they wanted you to do overtime, you did it willingly, because you wanted the little bit of extra money', said one woman who was an overlooker between 1923 and 1940. Overlookers literally scrutinised or looked over each completed piece of work, looking for any faults, checking that the item was properly sized and cutting off any loose ends of thread. Management was not so strict though about health and safety issues. A number of those interviewed describe painful experiences on the shop floor. A male corset worker who was employed for some forty years between approximately 1930 and 1970 remarked that 'more than one finger or thumb disappeared with the knife', presumably the knife used for cutting the heavy canvas material. Needles through fingers seem to have been commonplace. One poor girl working on the eyelet machine managed to put an eyelet right through the nail on her finger. One of her colleagues, a machinist between 1950 and 1957, recalled,

> they had to carry her down, she passed out, carry her down on a chair, the men in the factory had to come forwards and carry her down, and she went to hospital, I don't really know the outcome of that but there was blood all over the place it was awful really. They did tell us if you ... don't get a needle down your finger you're not a needlewoman.

Equally awful was what happened to the poor girl who caught her hair in her machine. One of her colleagues recalled that,

> she was getting married in three weeks' time! ... the [drive] band is at the side, underneath, and she bent down to pick up something, and of course that band is going round and round on the wheel, and she put her head down, and her hair caught in it ... . It took a piece of her hair out of her scalp. She had a nasty sore place there, and it was the shock, you know, the shock was more than anything.

Outworkers still had a place in the local workforce although the bulk of the manufacturing was undertaken on the shop floor. These were women who had been skilled factory workers, had married and were now raising families. Maureen Cook, a machinist between 1958 and 1971, worked at home for some two years or more until she had her son,

> and then I, when I had him, after a few months I tried to fit a bit in evenings and in the daytime when he was sleeping, but I used to keep to a day routine, even at home. I had a little bedroom that set up with a big bench machine ... I just kept to it as I would in the factory.

Doreen Kemp, a flat binder between 1945 and 1999, was an outworker for Celestrian Textiles which stood opposite Fratton Park football ground. As so many women had done before her, she collected her work from the nearby factory and then used her own family to help her,

> You had to go and collect all these straps, cut them, the elastic, thread them through the bar, then through the ring, stitch 'em and I had the whole family on them – the boys were treadling, I was stitching and John was cutting the elastic, I think!

Another woman was an overlooker and outworker for Berlei in the decade before the outbreak of the Second World War. She must have had some sort of connection previously with the firm which designed a new garment,

> and got it on the market and they wanted to get it out quick, they wanted me to go in the factory but I didn't want to go down in Portsmouth so my sister, her being a forewoman, persuaded them and, I think he was one of the managers, arranged for the work to be brought out to me and that was why I done it here for them and they paid me, collected it … only overlooking, I didn't do anything else.

Trying out new lines sometimes fell to the girls themselves. Doreen Kemp recalled with glee being invited to try out one of the 'very modern step-ins' [no laces],

> still in the tea rose, but they were made of nylon … which was very, very glamorous, then, you know … and I wore it for a couple of weeks, then I washed it by hand and then I had to take it back and show them how it had worn, just in a couple of weeks. But then I was allowed to keep it. That was all right!

Without exception the women interviewed enjoyed their work, as indeed did Mrs Le Santo. Admittedly they were for the most part working after 1945, but even those women whose working experience embraced the period between the two world wars speak fondly of their time in the factories. The financial pressure on dockyard wives and service families had eased after the First World War. There was work in the dockyard and allotted pay came through for service families. Women were no longer working simply to feed their families as they had done a hundred years before. After the First World War pensions were also paid to the dependants of men who had been killed or severely disabled in the fighting. In short, there was an acknowledged sufficiency for the bulk of the population which must account for the fact that Portsmouth with many of the characteristics of a northern industrial town and a large industrial working class supported the Conservatives locally and nationally for much of the twentieth century, unlike northern industrial centres.

In fact many of the cheerful faces in surviving photographs are of young women who have probably not yet married. There are photographs of peace celebrations on the factory floor in 1918, charabancs on works' outings from the early Twenties, and Christmas decorations and celebrations at the benches. Money was collected for wedding presents. They were small individual sums but put together purchased a memorable gift for the bride-to-be as Norah Channon, a machinist in the 1930s recalled,

> My wedding list, it's amazing. It is donations of 2d and 3d and even the mechanic gave me 9d so you can imagine how very restrictive our life was, but with that sum of money that they collected for me … it bought half a dinner service which I still got and a cheese dish that went with it and a crystal violet vase. We're talking about less than £3 I think.

Other girls speak of the 'brilliant' camaraderie,

> They all used to go out dancing the weekend. Fridays they'd sit there at their machines plucking their eyebrows, putting their hair in rollers, putting their turbans on …

and they'd all meet at The Savoy Friday nights and it was
the pier Saturday nights ... That's why I've always been
in a factory, I've always loved the life, it's so friendly.

When ships were in there were invitations to naval dances as
well, at The Savoy on Southsea seafront or, occasionally, on
Whale Island. Naval dances were keenly anticipated.

The First World War was the watershed, however, in terms
of female employment. It had an immediate and devastating
effect initially on women in local stay factories. The *Hampshire
Telegraph* carried a report on 21 August 1914 on the plight
of women affected by the sudden drop in orders. They faced
starvation. At one local factory five young female piece-workers
had only one hour's work on the day the paper's reporter called.
Their pay that week would amount to barely *2s 0d,* and they had
no idea how they would make ends meet. The wider implications
of their plight are discussed in the letter of local suffragist leader
Norah O'Shea to the *Evening News* on 29 August 1914. At a
meeting of the Civilian Sub-Committee of the Executive of
the National Relief Fund, held the following week, Councillor
Harold Pink, a prominent Portsmouth grocer, respected local
politician and three times mayor, suggested that some employers
whose male workers had been called up might usefully employ
corset girls in their place. Sir John Brickwood, chairman and
managing director of brewers Brickwood and Co. Ltd (founded
by his enterprising grandmother, Fanny Brickwood, c.1850)
stepped forward. His firm engaged thirty-two girls to take the
place of young men who had gone off to fight. 'It was the first
time', said Sir John, 'they had ever employed female labour...'.

In due course, as men enlisted, more women were recruited
to take over their work; work which had been considered in the
past well beyond their strength and capability. They took over
munitions work from men and after training in the Municipal
College, well over 1,000 girls went into local munitions factories.
Another 2,000 women replaced men in Portsmouth Dockyard,
undertaking clerical work initially but as increasing numbers
of men volunteered or were called up compulsorily, the

women moved into the different workshops. According to Gates, in his book *Portsmouth and the Great War,* which was published in 1919, women were employed across the dockyard,

> in the working of lathes, planing, shaping, milling, engraving, buffing...; in cleaning, cutting, and testing condenser tubes, making condenser ferrules, cleaning air bottles for submarines and ships; in general bench work and assisting the mechanics in cutting blades for condenser turbines. In the Boiler Shop they were engaged in acetylene welding, in cleaning, picking, galvanising, testing boiler tubes. Here also they were employed at lathes, drilling, screwing, punching and shearing machines. They also did small work on forges and assisted the mechanics on the automatic machines for bolts and nuts.

Women also worked in the Gun-Mounting Shop, in the Coppersmith's Shop, the Pattern

*Letter from Norah O'Shea, Secretary of the local branch of the NUWSS, to the* Evening News *urging local women sewing or knitting for soldiers 'to lay down their work', 29 August 1914. Portsmouth History Centre.*

# WAR LETTERS

## THE NEEDS OF WORKLESS WOMEN.

### A Plea to the Well-to-do.

[To the Editor of the "Evening News."]

Sir,—Many women have appealed to me to know what can be done to find them work. "Willing and able to work, and the war has taken away the living." I think there is one logical answer to that appeal, and I hope that soon the nation will rise to its responsibilities and insist that the need of the woman thrown out of a living by war is no less a charge upon it than the maintenance of the soldiers' and sailors' dependents. In the meantime I should like to support the appeal to all those engaged in sewing or knitting for soldiers, sailors or the needy, to lay down their work in order that it may be given to those whose living is threatened by the continuance of the war.

There is, I suppose, no greater trial for those willing and able to help than to stand by apparently useless. At a time like this it is the realities of life which must be faced, and perhaps the best sacrifice the well to do woman can make to-day is to deny herself personal service; to give up the work she desires to do in order that those who need may have the work, without which they cannot live.

It is not only the women in the factory, laundry, and dressmaking upon whom the stress of poverty has fallen, but the small trader, lodging-house keeper, florist, typist, clerk and domestic worker are all feeling the strain, and will soon be facing destitution. The daily Press calls the women to help, but if that help is to be real and effectual it must be given along right lines and supply the actual need, viz., work by which the woman can live. To stop sewing and knitting, or arranging sewing and knitting for others, does not mean that there is no place for the service of the well-to-do woman. Material and money will both be needed, and if all those now engaged in the actual work by making comforts for the troops and clothes for the destitute would guarantee an equivalent in material or money at least a start would be made. Pecuniarily just now the position of the soldier's or sailor's wife compares favourably with that of the woman in industry, and to do any work or fill any post for which the workless woman can be paid seems at a crisis like the present a denial of the desire to serve.

Yours faithfully,
N. O'SHEA.

Cosham.

Shop and Drawing Office. They turned capstans to move ships in basins, drove motor lorries, made overalls and flags, did electrical work on board ships, lacquered and zinc-coated baths, cleaned and painted the hulls of ships, sharpened saws and worked in the sawmills. There was anxiety at first about how easily the women would be integrated into the workforce. They had to put up with a lot of abuse to start with from their male colleagues. One woman recalled many years later that it was as well to carry an umbrella with you on the trams 'to give as good as you got', and to begin with the women left the dockyard before the men at the end of each day to limit aggressive behaviour but this distinction was soon dropped. Recalling what they did in later life, many spoke of this work experience as the happiest time of their lives. Like the girls in the stay factories a generation later, they enjoyed the company, the companionship and the friends made. They had money of their own, respect and were proud – of the badges they wore on war work, and the fact that much of what they had been doing was very demanding.

They had also coped successfully with the same problems their mothers had juggled with before them, and their daughters and granddaughters would continue to wrestle with long after the Second World War and, indeed, still wrestle with today: the difficulty of balancing the demands of both work and childcare. Those nursing babies spoke then of going home in their lunch breaks to feed the baby, cared for usually by paid help: a parent, neighbour or friend, although there was some limited nursery provision. However, they had coped, and they had proved that they could, one way or another, manage these competing demands. The implications were far-reaching.

Even before the First World War there is evidence in census records that Portsmouth women were quitting as indoor servants. Between 1901 and 1911 there was a fall of twelve per cent in the numbers employed. Those working in the dress trades continued to increase, albeit modestly, during this period but after the war they fell away and by 1931 were almost half their pre-war total. There was some consistency in the numbers of stay workers employed in the early twentieth century but by

*The following images show Portsmouth women at work in the dockyard during the First World War. Their triangular badges signify that they are on war work. Portsmouth Royal Dockyard Historical Trust.*

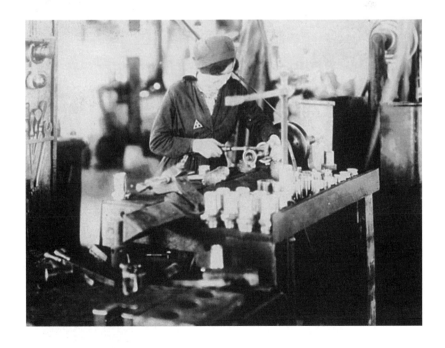

1951 their numbers had halved to just over 1,000 women and girls over the age of 15. Where did these departing women go – and why did they go? The census provides information on where they went. Why they went is another matter.

Census figures for nursing, teaching, work in central or local government, and retail and general office work are useful comparators and provide some of the answers. There were 519 female nurses and midwives working in the town in 1901, and 988 female teachers. There were also fifty-seven women employed in 'general' government, or central government as we would put it today, presumably this was clerical work in the dockyard or in the Post Office; seventy in local government, certainly in the Town Hall; and there were 282 working in commercial occupations as commercial or business clerks. By 1911 the numbers in these occupations were rising. There had been a modest increase in the numbers of nurses and midwives to 629. Teaching figures remained almost the same at 990 but those women working for central and local government had more than doubled to 124 and

129 respectively, as had the numbers employed as commercial and business clerks, which rose to 558.

By 1931 the story is clear. There is one new and particularly interesting statistic: 222 women were working in shipbuilding and repairing, and marine engineering, presumably in the dockyard although this is not made clear, and they must have been doing mechanical and engineering rather than clerical work, otherwise they would be tabulated under Public Administration and Defence. Under the actual headline of Public Administration and Defence there were 1,860 women of whom 214 were in the dockyard and 176 in the Post Office. As for local government, there were six women in the police force although it is not clear in what capacity, and there were 793 female teachers in local authority schools. Another 506 were working independently in private schools or as music, drama or art teachers. Women workers in the Town Hall are separately counted and number 474. Some 6,396 women were working in commerce and finance: in sweet shops, grocers, dairies, butchers, chemists' shops, drapers and department stores.

There were 376 women listed building ships, 628 working with motor vehicles and cycles, and 459 making aircraft parts in 1951. There were another 1,827 in Public Administration and Defence, 1,298 in central government jobs, presumably working in an administrative capacity on Admiralty and War Office sites, and 529 women in local government, working in the seafront hotels in Southsea requisitioned after the Guildhall was destroyed on the night of 10–11 January 1941. Nursing and teaching were brought together under Professional Services. Some 4,203 women altogether are accounted for beneath this headline. There were ninety working in accountancy, 1,163 teachers employed in both the local authority and independent sectors, 293 women in the legal profession, and 2,486 medical and dental workers. Of the 1,209 women in private domestic service, only 499 lived in, the remaining 710 were non-residential.

In just fifty years, female work patterns in Portsmouth had been revolutionised. Education had to have played some part. On 5 December 1870 the Borough Council adopted the

Elementary Education Act upon proof that there were 8,000 children in Portsmouth needing school accommodation and the next month the first elections took place to the School Board. Not a single woman though was elected to fill one of the 15 seats. A census was undertaken in March 1871 of the number of local children, male and female, between the ages of 3 and 13 needing education. There were 18,578. Six schools were opened initially in 1872 in different parts of the borough and within ten years the School Board had built accommodation for 9,000 children in twelve schools. There were still 11,000 children needing school places in 1880 and it was resolved to build a further two schools.

By the time the work of the School Board was transferred to the Borough Council in 1902 it had built twenty-six Elementary Schools and a Higher Grade School – for boys – which, with ten church or non-provided schools, could accommodate 30,890 children. A girls' secondary school was established in 1904 however, next door to the Higher Grade School which then became a secondary school. Secondary education would be fee-paying until 1944 but it is no coincidence that the revolution which took place in local female working patterns coincided with a similar revolution in the provision of elementary education which was free from 1870 and compulsory from 1880 for 5 to 10 year-olds.

The school-leaving age rose in stages from 12 in 1899 to 14 in 1918. Eighty per cent of children left after elementary education but the twenty per cent who remained in secondary education and, it is probably safe to say, a fair number of those who had to leave school at the age of 14 and put on hold any academic ambitions, had their eyes opened in school to possibilities beyond the confines of life in domestic service or in a dress factory. However, in any consideration of female trades and occupations, it must be remembered that even as late as 1951 only twenty-two per cent of the total number of females in the local population actually worked in paid employment. During the nineteenth century, most women did not work. They kept house and raised families. Without any domestic assistance and before the introduction of any labour-saving devices, this was a full-time job.

## CHAPTER FOUR

# 'Neat, trim and taut...'

# ✳✳✳

There was a picture in the *Illustrated London News* on 19 August 1893 with the title 'On the Parade, Southsea'. Set possibly behind Southsea Castle, it is an image of a confident young woman stepping out in a smart boater, her loosely-tied neck scarf catching the breeze and her gloved hands controlling a parasol which, in the breeze, threatens to acquire a life of its own. She wears a neat jacket with a nipped-in waist. Her skirt is just above her ankles and she wears a pretty pair of court shoes decorated with bows. Is it really high season? All the parties in the picture are well wrapped-up and the small dog, trotting behind, presumably belonging to her, wears a coat too!

Perhaps it was the sort of summer described by Clement Scott who spent a wet and depressing summer holiday on Hayling Island c.1897. He felt he had been imprisoned,

> Not a vestige of blue sky by day, or a golden star by night ... The Isle of Wight was completely blotted out. Spithead and its forts were in tears. The Warner light could not flash through the grey gloom, and after dinner, pacing the conservatory of the 'Bungalow Yacht', it was impossible for three long imprisoned evenings to see the welcome illumination on Southsea Pier.

His joy knew no bounds however when the rain cleared finally – on the very day of the Southsea Regatta. Of Southsea, he said,

*'On the Parade, Southsea' from the* Illustrated London News, *19 August, 1893. Author's Collection.*

there is one peculiarity. It is smart! The girls, he wrote, were 'neat, trim and taut' and,

> half of them [are] the daughters or relations of retired army and navy men, and they would not have a ribbon or buckle out of place for the world. All the girls at Southsea appear to be under the eye of the commanding officer, and always 'at attention'. It is the headquarters of primness and pipeclay.

As for Southsea Common and the seafront, he reckoned you could get as fine a breath of fresh air there as you could wish, 'for does not Southsea boast a sea-wall, embankment, and promenade all round and about the old castle, a sea-front and

*Ladies Mile, and Clarence Parade, c.1906. Author's Collection.*

esplanade nearly as fine as Eastbourne?' The young lady in the picture clearly thought so – and is, indubitably, 'on parade'. She cuts a very different figure to the girls who sought sanctuary in one of the local refuges or homes for fallen women which were located not so far away.

More usually middle-class Southsea ladies in the last decade of the nineteenth century were featured 'on parade' on Sunday mornings after church in photographs and picture postcards of the tree-lined Ladies Mile on Southsea Common. Ladies Mile ran parallel with Clarence Parade from its junction with South Parade almost to the Queen's Hotel. The promenaders and their daughters lived lives a world apart from those of most of the women and girls of the old town of Portsmouth, Portsea and Landport. Clement Scott observed correctly when he said that many of the girls he admired were the daughters or relations of navy and army officers. They were also the wives and daughters of senior dockyard officials and local business and professional men. In fact, Ray Riley calculated in 'The Houses and Inhabitants of Thomas Ellis Owen's Southsea' that in the census years 1851 and 1861 naval and military officers, active and retired, made up almost half the heads of households in the heart of historic Southsea which Owen himself played a key role developing over a thirty-year period between roughly 1830 and 1870, actually building St Jude's Church on the corner of Kent Road, at its junction with Grove Road South, to attract new residents. For many years it was the town's smartest church, a 'carriage' church, and the venue for any number of naval and military weddings, as the parish registers and the reports in local newspapers attest. St Jude's was at the heart of Southsea and encircled by the streets which Owen built: Elm Grove, Queen's Crescent, Kent Road and Portland Road; Grove Road and Palmerston Road; The Thicket, Nelson Road and Albany Road; Clarendon Road and The Circle; The Vale and Villiers Road; the Eastern Villas Road area and Florence Road. Many of the houses survive to this day and it would have been in one of these houses that young women, like the girl 'on parade', lived.

These houses were spacious, well-ventilated and usually had their own gardens. Large villas and terraces built by Owen in Kent Road, Sussex Road and Queen's Crescent and the adjoining streets had drawing rooms, breakfast rooms, dining rooms and studies. Wide staircases led upstairs to bedrooms, dressing rooms, nursery accommodation and, at the top of narrower flights of stairs, to rooms beneath the eaves where live-in staff slept. A feature of the early villas and terraces was provision of sluices in maids' cleaning cupboards on the first floor for the quick and easy dispatch to subterranean drains of the contents of chamber pots and wash basins. Plumbed bathing spaces i.e. bathrooms were not yet standard features in such properties. There was no city-wide drainage system either at this stage in the town's life, but builders such as Owen devised their own local drainage schemes. Owen also laid on a fresh water supply from his own wells in nearby King's Road. Basement or semi-basement space was allocated to domestic offices: kitchens, sculleries, china stores, larders and food storage, wine cellars, laundry facilities, and a room for the servants to eat in and rest during the day (this space was not quite large enough to be dignified with the description Servants' Hall). There was also staff privy accommodation. Interestingly Owen provided very little stabling even though coachmen do feature on the census returns in some instances. Horses and carriages were usually hired from firms like the Southsea Carriage Company in nearby Auckland Road.

A local politician and businessman as well as a builder, Owen (he was twice Mayor of Portsmouth before his death in 1862) was Southsea's first and most famous architect. Altogether he built some 106 villas and 54 terraced houses in what Pevsner in his 'Hampshire' volume of *The Buildings of England* describes rather scathingly as 'odd variants of late Regency or Early Victorian styles'. However, these landmark cottages *ornés,* stucco villas and terraces, artfully designed, and landscaped to maximise impact, attracted notice. People wanted to live in them and other local builders soon followed suit with similar properties. They included Henry Francis Gauntlett, an architect and surveyor, and also a local timber and coal merchant; Isaac Moody, another timber merchant, and builders like John Aylen and Charles Braxton. 'Odd variants', these properties may have been but the quality and variety of Owen's housing and that of his contemporaries was never achieved again on the same scale in Southsea.

Pressure on building land, driven by dockyard expansion, and the prospect of better profits on your investment, saw a return once again, as the century progressed, to what Patricia Haskell has called 'Portsmouth's customary cramped monotony' of 'straight rows of large or small red-brick houses tailored to the occupants' income.' These are properties built to the east of Victoria Road and nearer the seafront where infilling took place in middle-class strongholds behind South Parade and in a series of roads built to the west of Owen's own home, Dovercourt, south of Kent Road. Clement Scott was not over worried by these developments,

> Municipally considered, I don't suppose that there are two smarter sea-coast places in the south than Southsea

and Portsmouth. Everything for the public service, such as cabs and lighting and good roads and order, is admirably managed at both places; but I very much doubt if 'old salts' would recognise the Portsmouth of Charles Dickens and Captain Marryat ... in the new, smart, red-bricked Portsmouth.

As discussed already, this was a society dominated by women, a significant number of whom were young female servants but there was another reason why women outnumbered men within many mid-nineteenth century families. Put simply, it was because well-bred girls stayed at home until they married and such were the restrictions imposed on them that many never married. Riley cites several households with ageing, unmarried daughters such as that of Mr H.W. Ross who was 78 years old and a fundholder living at 5 Portland Terrace in 1861. He had four daughters living at home aged 41, 39, 26 and 22, and four female servants. Vice Admiral Henry Chads next door had three daughters living with him aged 40, 38 and 33.

Significant numbers of women in Owen's Southsea were also fundholders i.e. they lived off investments. Riley calculated that in 1851, eighteen of the twenty-eight heads of households he sampled who were property owners, fundholders or annuitants were women, and ten years later in 1861 they numbered thirty out of thirty-six. He did a further exercise in which he used the number of servants employed as a surrogate for income and demonstrated that many of these financially-independent ladies were living in considerable style,

> Several boasted two or three servants but the 1851 census records Margaret Hall living in Queen's Terrace supported by four servants including a butler, Amelia Otter residing at Eastlands with a similar retinue, and even more ostentatiously, Lady Lennox inhabiting Portland Terrace with no less than five servants at her disposal.

Lady Harriet Blackwood of Nelson Villa, and The Honourable Maria Byng and her daughter, Beatrice, a maid of honour to

HM the Queen, who lived in Queen's Terrace, had four servants apiece in 1861.

Riley also proved that the concentration of wealthy householders in Southsea contributed significantly to the town's position as the fifth wealthiest town in the country in the mid-nineteenth century, by relating the size of the local population to the amount they paid in assessed taxation. Thus he demonstrated that in 1847–8, some 49,214 Portsmouth people paid £18,059 in assessed taxation, i.e. £0.37 per head which was the fifth highest sum after Bath (£0.59), Cheltenham (£0.57), Brighton (£0.55), and London (£0.42). It must be remembered too that the inclusion of the entire local population in this calculation must have depressed the Portsmouth figure significantly. What these statistics actually prove is that by the mid-nineteenth century Southsea was a sought-after residential area with a significant preponderance of women in its midst: female residential servants; the wives and daughters of the navy and military, and local business and professional men; and the widows of such men, of independent means, and living in some style in the grander terraces and villas of Owen's Southsea. But aside from the female servants what were these women doing all day?

Some women wrote! It was an honourable calling which, if she needed money to make ends meet, an educated woman might reasonably pursue. Several women who were either born in Portsmouth or spent time living here became successful authors, and this tradition continues to the present day. An early writer who was born in the town, according to David Francis in his recent survey of Portsmouth novelists, was Susanna Haswell Rowson who was baptised in St Thomas's Church in 1762 and became the United States's first best-selling novelist. She was raised partly in Massachusetts where her father was a customs collector. However, the family returned to England in 1778 after war broke out with the American colonists. Susanna was employed initially as a governess, and began to write. Her first novel, *Victoria,* was published in 1786, and in 1791 *Charlotte* was published. It was not particularly successful in this country.

She returned with her husband to the newly-established United States and settled in Boston. *Charlotte* was reissued and was an enormous success for its author. It is a cautionary tale of a woman led astray. The story begins in Chichester and the parties sailed from Portsmouth to America where most of the action takes place.

The author Sarah Doudney was more typical of the women who lived in Owen's Southsea. She was born in Portsmouth in 1841 and baptised at St Mary's Church, Portsea. Her family owned a prosperous candle and soap manufactory in Landport, near the Royal Portsmouth, Portsea and Gosport Hospital. She was educated in Southsea and certainly lived at some point in Grove Road, in the heart of this area. She did not need to write. Presumably she enjoyed doing so and, given the nature of her output, she felt she had some sort of vocation. She was no Mrs Gaskell but during her long life she wrote many hymns, religious poems and novels. *The Great Salterns* was published by The Religious Tract Society in 1875 and is a moral tale set in and around a house of that name on Portsea Island. Sarah Doudney died in 1926. Olivia Manning was also born in Portsmouth, at 134, Laburnum Grove in 1908, into an impoverished naval family. She was educated locally and began her working life in a Portsmouth architect's office but escaped to London as soon as she could. Her best known works are the semi-autobiographical Balkan and Levant trilogies published between 1960 and 1980 and memorably dramatised for television in 1987 starring Kenneth Branagh and Emma Thompson.

More usually the women who lived in Owen's Southsea kept house, and it was a full-time job in a large household. It is no coincidence that the opening chapter of *Mrs Beeton's Book of Household Management* is devoted to 'The Mistress' and the first sentence is a quotation from the Bible, Proverbs 21:25–8, in gothic script, doubtless to emphasise the sanctity of the sentiments,

> Strength and honour are her clothing; and she shall rejoice in time to come. She openeth her mouth with wisdom; and in her tongue is the law of kindness. She

looketh well to the ways of her household; and eateth
not the bread of idleness. Her children arise up, and call
her blessed; her husband also, and he praiseth her.

Thus the tone was set for a book, published originally in parts
but brought together first in one set of covers in 1861. It proved
to be a best-seller and, heavily revised over the years to reflect
changing times, and views, is still in print. The opening salvo of
the 1861 edition is followed by the first of a series of attributes
to be expected of the virtuous mistress of a household. The
first principle adumbrated is that the mistress of a household
must be like the commander of an army or indeed leader of
any enterprise. On the efficiency with which she undertakes
her domestic duties will depend 'the happiness, comfort, and
well-being of a family'. This should not preclude, however,
the enjoyment of 'proper pleasures or amusing recreation'.
The 'home qualities and virtues which are necessary to the
proper management of a Household' included early rising,
cleanliness (the person and the house), frugality and economy,
the careful choice of acquaintances, cautious commitment to
new friendships, and hospitality, 'but care must be taken that
the love of company, for its own sake, does not become a
prevailing passion; for then the habit is no longer hospitality,
but dissipation'. There are also recommendations on how to
conduct a conversation and what not to share with the hearer,
on cultivating an even temper at all times, and advice on how to
dress. Dress should be adapted to your circumstances and 'be
varied with different occasions',

> Thus, at breakfast she [the mistress of the household]
> should be attired in a very neat and simple manner,
> wearing no ornaments. If this dress should decidedly
> pertain only to the breakfast-hour, and be specially
> suited for such domestic occupations as usually follow
> that meal, then it would be well to exchange it before the
> time for receiving visitors, if the mistress be in the habit
> of doing so. It is still to be remembered, however, that,

in changing the dress, jewellery and ornaments are not to be worn until the full dress for dinner is assumed.

Additional advice is dispensed on charity and benevolence which Mrs Beeton declares are 'duties which a mistress owes to herself as well as to her fellow-creatures; and there is scarcely any income so small, but something may be spared from it, even if it be but 'the widow's mite'. There is also an instructive piece on visiting the poor which is described as the only practical way to properly understand the plight of families,

> and although there may be difficulties in following out this plan in the metropolis and other large cities, yet in country towns and rural districts these objections do not obtain. Great advantages may result from visits paid to the poor; for there being, unfortunately, much ignorance, generally, amongst them with respect to all household knowledge, there will be opportunities for advising and instructing them, in a pleasant and unobtrusive manner, in cleanliness, industry, cookery, and good management.

More useful tips follow on marketing, and the general recommendation that usually 'the best articles are the cheapest'. Further it is suggested that unless you have an 'experienced and confidential' housekeeper, you should undertake the provisioning of your household yourself. Proper accounts should be kept at all times. Engaging servants, their treatment and the giving of a character, merit a number of detailed paragraphs – and thus the advice for the efficient management of the household continues for another thirty additional paragraphs.

This is precisely what was expected of all leisured middle-class women in the mid-nineteenth century. In fact it was an expectation of all married women. Their capacity to undertake the tasks outlined was limited solely by the assets available to them, as struggling housewives in Portsea and Landport, and Mrs Price and Mrs Knapp certainly, could attest feelingly. Few original accounts survive of what life was like locally at the upper end of the social scale. However, there is the diary of Georgiana

Clarke-Jervoise, the wife of Jervoise Clarke-Jervoise. She came to old Idsworth Park, a few miles north-east of Portsmouth, as a young wife in 1834, and she kept her diary for five years between 1863 and 1868. It is in the Hampshire Record Office in Winchester. The house's proximity to the new railway line prompted the family's removal to a new brick-built mansion in 1851, some two miles away, but this did not affect their very comfortable lives. Georgiana says little about her husband's activities. He was in fact a landowner of some substance, a Justice of the Peace, Deputy Lieutenant, and the Member of Parliament for South Hampshire 1857–68. Almost nothing is said in the diary either about Georgiana's domestic duties as mistress of a household which included seven female and four male servants. There are some references to the French and German governesses who occupied a more elevated position in the household. There is also information about going to London to interview candidates for the position of her personal maid, and some detail about servants' balls which were held

*Idsworth House. Designed by William Burn in 1851 for Jervoise Clarke-Jervoise. Author's Collection.*

to celebrate Christmas and particularly noteworthy occasions such as a family wedding when dancing often went on until the early hours of the morning.

Blessed fortunately with a family of two sons and four daughters who seem to have enjoyed robust good health, Georgiana was able to devote her energies to their upbringing and the family's social life. The whole family, the women included, were enthusiastic huntsmen. They also enjoyed shooting. Georgiana records with pride the first occasion her small grandson, Arthur, went out with the guns at the age of 11 in 1868. He hunted for the first time some two years earlier when he was blooded and was presented with the brush. Georgiana herself does not seem to have hunted. Her own preferred activity was croquet, and in August 1866 she recorded eleven croquet parties attended in the neighbourhood and her own at Idsworth Park on 22 August when she entertained eighty-three neighbours.

She records meticulously and with clear pleasure all who came to stay, and who came to lunch or dine. Visitors are a roll-call of the local big houses and their occupants: Sir William and Lady Knighton from Blendworth Lodge and Sir Michael Seymour from Cadlington House, Horndean. From further afield came the Jervoises from Herriard near Basingstoke, the Scotts from Rotherfield Park, East Tisted and the families from Government House and Admiralty House in Portsmouth. Their visitors returned invitations. There were dinners, and regimental and naval balls, in Portsmouth (and trips to Mr Martin, the dentist, in the High Street). They were guests too at Stansted House, Rowlands Castle, and Rookesbury Park at Wickham, as well as Uppark at South Harting, and they attended a ball at Goodwood House on the occasion of Lord March's coming-of-age celebrations on 27 January 1867.

Georgiana also describes two major naval events in Portsmouth attended by parties from Idsworth Park. The first was the occasion of the Visit of the French Fleet to Portsmouth in August 1865. The town was *en fête* and, according to Gates, all the time the ships lay at Spithead there were numerous social

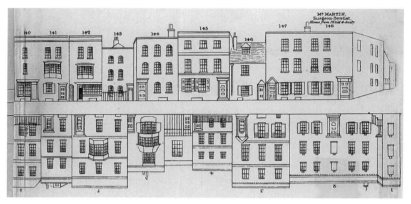

*Surgeon Dentist Mr Martin's premises at 148, High Street, Portsmouth (they would have been opposite the Cambridge Barracks built in 1856 and now part of Portsmouth Grammar School) from* The Stranger's Guide; or Charpentier's Engraved Street View, *c.1845. Author's Collection.*

## THE TEETH !

### MESSRS. HAY & HAZEL

Have the honor and privilege of introducing to their Friends, the following select remedies for preserving the Teeth and Gums in a sound and healthy state: they are the result of Mr. Martin's experience, during his practice in Dental Surgery, and Messrs H. & H. assure their friends, that they are prepared with their usual accuracy and care.

### COMPOUND
## CAMPHORATED TOOTH POWDER,

*As prescribed by Mr. Martin, Surgeon-Dentist.*

148, HIGH-STREET, PORTSMOUTH.

The action of Dentifrice should be in the generality of cases slightly *mechanical*, to assist in removing any discoloration or incrustation ; *medicinal*, to render the Gums firm and healthy by diminishing tenderness and imparting tone and vigour ; *chemical*, to neutralize any corrosive agent that may be retained or generated in the mouth, either by the decomposition of animal or vegetable substances. Mr. Martin has not lost sight of these objects in prescribing the Compound Camphorated Tooth Powder, which should be used with the Improved Tooth Brushes twice daily. A small quantity should be put in an earthenware or china box.

Sold by Messrs. Hay & Hazel, Chemists, &c. No. 53, High-street, Portsmouth, in bottles of 2s. 6d. each, with directions for use.

## THE TEETH !

### CONCENTRATED
## ESSENCE OF CAMPHOR,

AS PRESCRIBED BY

*Mr. Martin, Surgeon-Dentist,*

No. 148, HIGH-STREET, PORTSMOUTH.

Camphor has long been recommended by the most eminent practitioners in Dental Surgery, both in England and France, as a valuable and efficacious remedy for constringing and imparting tone to the Gums. Spirits of Camphor is the form in which it has been ordered, but when mixed with water for the purpose of forming a mouth wash, the Camphor is instantly returned to a concrete state and is seen floating on the surface, consequently the water *is merely impregnated with the odour of Camphor.* The Concentrated Essence on the contrary is misable with *soft water*, holding the Camphor in Solution *with all its properties.*

Sold by Messrs. Hay & Hazel, Chemists, &c. No. 53, High-street, Portsmouth, in bottles of 2s. 6d., 5s., and 10s. each, with directions for use.

### PRESERVATIVE DENTIFRICE.

This Tooth Powder is found invaluable when the Gums are relaxed and receding ; it causes them to embrace the teeth, rendering those that are slightly loose *firm* and *useful.* It is a powerful antiseptic, and not only corrects, but prevents any disagreeable odour, and im-

N 5.

*An early example of an advertorial: tooth powders prescribed by Mr Martin advertised in a mid-nineteenth century guide. Author's Collection.*

occasions taking place on shore for the visitors. Georgiana reported in her diary that the fleet was lit up at night and they made up a party of three carriages, including the Vicar of Blendworth, Mr Astley, to drive into Portsmouth, where they had been invited to go on board the *Fire* by Sir Richard Seymour, to view the scene. Two years later on 17 July 1867 another party went down to Portsmouth to see the Fleet Review in honour of the Sultan of Turkey who was visiting the port. If it had been possible to see the spectacle it would have been a grand sight: eight wooden frigates, two wooden sloops, fifteen iron or ironclad frigates and sloops, sixteen gunboats, five Royal yachts, eighteen troopships, yachts and tenders – but the weather was atrocious. 'Some of our party went to Lumps Fort', noted Georgiana, 'the rest to Hayling Island. No one at either place saw anything'.

However, the highlight of each year for Georgiana was the London season. She decamped with the girls to their London town house for as long as four months at a time between February and June. The girls had dancing lessons and went on educational visits to museums and art galleries, the zoo and horticultural events. Most evenings were spent at the theatre, opera or a musical performance, a lecture or reading, and in her diary Georgiana notes assiduously the names of the performers and the particulars of the productions they saw. Whether her three eldest daughters met their husbands during the London season, we do not know, but Georgiana notes with satisfaction in her diary the marriages of the three eldest between 1863 and 1868.

We also learn there that she did exercise a benevolent oversight of village life. She visited the school and twice a year she arranged for the village children's hair to be cut by a Mr Cole. There were fifty-four children and the exercise cost 12 shillings. She organised a school clothing club and gave a Christmas tea each year for the women and children. Each July a treat was held in the park of the old house from noon to 11 o'clock in the evening. Up to 400 people were known to have attended on occasion. The marriage of the Prince of Wales on 10 March 1863 was celebrated with a dinner at Chalton for labourers and their wives, a tea party in Clanfield and the distribution of a shilling a head in Idsworth to all labourers and their families. A bonfire on Windmill Down brought the day's celebrations to a satisfactory conclusion.

Whether this was the complete extent of Georgiana's philanthropic endeavours, we do not know, but there was widespread giving by the local political elite during the nineteenth and early twentieth centuries, and charities, large and small, were dominated by – and heavily dependent on – middle-class, well-heeled men and women with the time and the money to devote to them. As Mrs Beeton advised, and the clergy preached from their pulpits, it was your duty to alleviate the suffering of your fellow-citizens. There was also of course some satisfaction to be obtained from seeing your name on a subscription list with a generous sum of money alongside.

Many local charities established in the first half of the nineteenth century were associated with one or other of the local churches. The Portsea Compassionate Society which visited the old and the sick was a good example. It was linked to St John's Portsea which was an evangelical parish where Mrs Knapp's husband, the Reverend John Knapp, ministered from 1853 until his death in 1881. His large, enthusiastic and growing (but mainly middle-class) congregation played its part in running a Bible class for young women which had a membership of 120, as well as a Bible class for young men of about sixty to seventy members which became the nucleus of the Portsea Island Young Men's Christian Association (YMCA) established by John Knapp. In his efforts to reach the working-class men and women in his parish he launched the Circus Church in a vacant circus building in Landport. The experimental gospel services attracted huge congregations from the first night in June 1857 when over 2,000 people crowded into the building. However, all three agents of the revival in the fortunes of the Anglican Church in the nineteenth century: the Evangelicals, the Anglo-Catholics and the middle-of-the-road Anglican clergy, such as Edgar Jacob, Cosmo Gordon Lang and Garbett at St Mary's Portsea, recruited the energies of their congregations to tackle pastoral issues and social concerns as the century progressed. Middle-class women played a key role in much of this charitable activity. Volunteers were needed because there were simply not enough clergymen to tackle the work which needed to be done. Lay involvement was vital. The women who volunteered did not need to work for their living and were recruited from the 1860s to do Sunday School teaching, parish visiting, to run a wide range of societies and clubs for women and children particularly, to manage soup kitchens and clothing clubs, and of course to raise money. They were indispensable to the delivery of these initiatives, although men were still involved in their management.

Christian evangelism inspired several notable women who worked in Portsmouth in the mid- to late nineteenth century. Mary Colebrook is a good example. She was a widow in 1862 with a young child, a girl, who would in due course succeed her as Superintendent of the Home with which she came to be so closely associated. Mary's husband, George, had been a businessman in Queen Street, Portsea, and he seems to have left her generously provided for. It is also possible that she worshipped at this stage in her life at St John's Church, Portsea as she later became an enthusiastic worshipper at the Circus Church in Landport, established by John Knapp to better address the needs of the working-class members of St John's parish. She is described by Field as a 'penitentiary activist' which is a fair description. By 1863 she was running a small Home she had opened herself in King Street, Portsmouth when she was asked to take over the running of the nearby penitentiary, as it was called then, in Brunswick Road. According to her obituary, the penitentiary 'was in need of such vitality as she, with her zeal and energy, was able to infuse into it, for it was in a parlous state'. She closed down the Home in King Street and brought with her to Brunswick Road the young women then in residence. There she began work for the Portsmouth Rescue Society and Protestant Home for Fallen Women as it was renamed on 1 May 1863 'without salary or monetary reward' and enjoyed conspicuous success for some thirty years.

The 1894 Annual Report, the thirty-first, brought together the numerous obituaries published in local newspapers following her death on 16 October 1893. The *Evening News* reported that,

> In undertaking the role of Lady Superintendent, Mrs Colebrook took over the entire management and control of the Institution, and became responsible for the funds therewith to carry it on. Not only did she give her time and labour to the work, but she spent her money freely on it as well and, although for more than eighteen years past she had been in ill-health, which at times confined her to her bed, it was not until within the last eighteen months that she had perforce resigned the management into the hands of Miss Colebrook, her only child. The good results of Mrs Colebrook's devoted labours have come before the public from time to time, in spite of the quiet and unostentatious manner in which the work was always carried on. At the Police-court every now and then the value of her work would be made manifest when an errant one whom the Magistrates hesitated to send to gaol had to be taken charge of. Mrs Colebrook was also a frequent visitor at Kingston Prison, where her ministrations and her practical help were productive of lasting good to many of the poor inmates. Midnight meetings and visits to fallen women at their lodgings have been among the means used for inducing them to enter the Home, where they were afterwards given laundry and other kinds of work and subjected to religious instruction and moral influence.

At the time of her death there were thirty-five residents but, according to the *Hampshire Post*, over the thirty-year period Mrs Colebrook was in charge, some 3,285 women entered the Home – although some were readmissions. After training, 1,142 women were sent into service or situations, 669 were sent to friends and relatives, 370 were sent to other Homes, Hospitals and Unions, ten were sent abroad, and twenty-six were actually married from the Home. Some 966 left at their own request, but the paper was anxious to assure its readers that this did not imply that the women were not doing well or had returned to the streets. What it usually meant was that the women had gone to friends or situations which they had found themselves. The paper also touched on Mrs Colebrook's own strong faith,

> The sturdiest and best morality, as Milton testifies in one of his immortal lines, is the morality which is the fruit of godliness. Herself a believer in the old Gospel, Mrs Colebrook presented it to those committed to her care (Mrs Colebrook and the inmates of her Home were for years attendants at the Circus Church); and it was her unspeakable happiness to have been the instrument of turning many to righteousness. With it all, she was a woman of quiet spirit and lowly mind; without show and parade, in a day in which glitter and noise pass for a good deal; of a large and open heart and motherly instincts, never more happy than when seeking and saving the waifs and strays of the town, and cheering all within her reach in their distress.

This writer also alluded to the help she gave to the Justices by taking in young women who came up before them whom they did not wish to send to gaol. There is also reference to the many tokens of affection she received each year on New Year's Day and on May Day, the anniversary of her taking over the home, not only from her domestic staff and the current residents, but also from former inmates, their families and friends. Two small account books survive in the Portsmouth History Centre in Mrs Colebrook's own handwriting covering the period 1869 to 1893. They record the income received – in cash and in kind – each month from a wide range of sources. On average a sum ranging from £23 0s 0d – £35 0s 0d came in each month from the regular subscribers to the Rescue Society. The Circus Church and other local churches also sent sums raised by special collections. More sums came from members of the public, a number of whom remained anonymous. A sum of £2 0s 0d was noted on 25 February 1874 as,

> A thank offering from one who has been brought to know the Saviour since she entered the Home August 10 1866 at the age of 17 years, was married from the Institution 3 years since.

There are in fact a number of gifts noted, for modest sums, from grateful former residents. Gifts in kind for the House included clothing, dress materials, meat, fish, fruit and vegetables. At Christmas time there were substantial gifts of raisins, currants and candied peel, and canisters of spices. Trustees, officers and committee members gave money towards the Christmas dinner. In the summer months came gallons of strawberries and raspberries, bushels of gooseberries, and lbs of blackcurrants and redcurrants from well-wishers. Mrs Colebrook was poorly in May 1873 and noted that during her sickness she received gifts of new laid eggs, oysters, jellies, oranges, strawberries, chicken and asparagus. Each anonymous gift had a 'portion' of scripture, as she called it, attached such as the following,

> The Lord bless thee and keep thee. The Lord make his face to shine upon thee and be gracious unto thee; The Lord lift up his countenance upon thee and give thee peace. Numbers 6 24-26.

By the time she died, the Home had moved again, to new, purpose-built premises in Hyde Park Road, on the corner of Commercial Road and Waltham Street. The *Hampshire Post* explained in its obituary that Rescue Society subscribers had presented Mrs Colebrook with the site and its old building; and within a very short period of time a splendid red-brick building had risen in its place, clear of all debt, 'the sum needed being chiefly sent in, in answer to prayer, in two sums of £900 and £300 each'. The paper added that the contributions from her own purse towards the maintenance of the Home 'must during her thirty years' superintendence have been very considerable'. The laundry on the new building's premises where the inmates worked was the financial mainstay of the institution. Revenue also came from the restaurant on the corner of the new building which had been sub-let to Messrs Shepherd and Co., the Railway Carriers, and the Private Hotel with its Coffee Room and eight beds which was managed and operated by staff of the Home. The organisation of the Home had been transformed in thirty years. It was now vested in six individual trustees and nine officers, all male, a General Committee of twenty-two, again all male, and a Ladies Committee of thirty-six. There was a separate Committee and Band of Workers for Midnight Meetings and Rescuing Work of thirty-six members, twenty-four of whom were women. It is possible to identify among their number, as might be expected, the wives and daughters of local clergymen, business and civic leaders, and naval and military men. Few of them could have had any illusions about the problems faced by many of their less fortunate sisters.

There were other key individuals doing rescue work in the town besides Mrs Colebrook. They included Mother Emma who belonged to the Community of St Andrew (CSA). The CSA was an Anglican religious order of professed sisters in holy orders or in diaconal ministry which was founded in London in 1861. Their early work was the training of young women as deaconesses for parish work, nursing and teaching, initially in London parishes but in due course they supplied sisters to work in other dioceses. Emma Day became a probationer in London on 14 April 1873 and made her profession as a deaconess on 3 December 1874. She was sent to work in the Diocese of Winchester and in 1879 the Winchester Diocesan Deaconess Home opened in Farnham with Sister Emma as its Head Deaconess. It moved to Portsmouth in 1884. She worked tirelessly to raise the money required to establish a permanent home for the deaconesses at 99–105 Victoria Road North in Southsea. This was St Andrew's Home. She and her fellow-workers were also indefatigable in their efforts to support

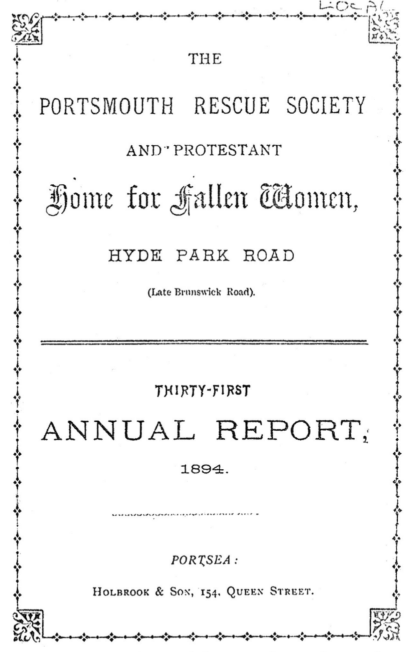

*Covers of the 31st Annual Report of The Portsmouth Rescue Society and Protestant Home for Fallen Women, 1894. Portsmouth History Centre.*

women and girls on the streets who wanted to turn their lives round, as the Diocesan Case Books show.

By 1894 there were altogether thirty-seven deaconess sisters, probationers and resident female church workers. By 1901 there were sixteen deaconesses and twenty-five lay women of whom one deaconess and twelve lay women were on the staff of St Mary's, Portsea. When Mother Emma died in 1920 Gates wrote in *Records of the Corporation*,

> By the death of 'Mother Emma' in February, the religious life of Portsmouth suffered heavy loss. From the early eighties [sic] she was the leading churchwoman and one of the most notable social workers of the diocese. In 1889 Portsmouth was chosen for the permanent home of the Deaconesses, and the large sum of money necessary for the building of St Andrew's Home at Southsea was raised through her personal efforts. It has since become one of the great centres of social work and of the Church and intellectual life of the town and diocese. Mother Emma's whole life was spent in service, and she ever displayed a rare spirit of comradeship and understanding charity.

There were only nine deaconesses and four lay workers by the time war broke out in 1939. Afterwards they moved to smaller premises in Southsea but their numbers continued to decline due probably to a combination of things: declining vocations and what can best be described as the centralisation and municipalisation of social care after 1947. St Andrew's Home was closed in 1958 and in due course its funds went into a trust for women's ministerial training.

The last deaconess working in Portsmouth, Deaconess Ada, who was attached to the former parish church, now the cathedral, was ordained deacon in 1994 at the same time as the first group of Portsmouth women were ordained to the priesthood. There is a three-fold ordained order in the Anglican ministry of bishops, priests and deacons. Ada was elderly by this time and did not seek to be ordained subsequently to the priesthood but she continued to undertake pastoral care and community work, as she and her fellow-sisters had always done, until ill-health persuaded her to retire. However, something still survives of the work of the deaconesses in Portsmouth. Mother Emma founded a nursing home, the Home of Comfort for the Dying, in 1896, in the heart of Owen's Southsea. It opened originally with just twelve residents. Highly regarded, the Home of Comfort (the words 'for the Dying' were later dropped) now offers care to twenty-nine older people with long-term and palliative nursing needs, and is still closely linked to local churches.

Another woman who followed what might also be described as a religious calling was Agnes Weston who founded the Royal Sailors' Rests in Devonport and Portsmouth. Born in 1840, she was the daughter of a barrister. Her father retired in 1845 and moved his family to Bath. Agnes was educated there and prepared for confirmation by the Reverend James Fleming, curate at St Stephen Lansdown in the parish of Walcot, Bath between 1855 and 1859. Presented to St Michael's Chester Square in London in 1873, Fleming would become a well-known public speaker, a canon of York Minster and a chaplain to both Queen Victoria and King Edward VII. His plain evangelical preaching in his Bath parish attracted large congregations and strongly influenced the teenage Agnes. She took up hospital visiting and parish work and, doubtless inspired by Fleming who was a total abstainer, began speaking at temperance meetings. She opened a coffee bar for soldiers of the 2nd Somerset Militia Brigade and when they were posted away, kept in touch with them by letter. She was asked in due course to correspond with a steward on board a troopship and from these very simple beginnings, her work with the Royal Navy developed in partnership with her good friend Sophia Wintz.

Born in Switzerland, Sophia came to England after her father died. Her brother, Lewis, joined the Royal Navy and rose to the rank of Vice-Admiral. Sophia was educated at a school near Fareham, just outside Portsmouth. While staying at Bath she met Agnes and they became close friends. They began holding Sunday afternoon meetings in Plymouth, at Sophia's mother's house for boys from the training ships in Devonport. The perils of drink featured largely in these gatherings and from them grew the idea of establishing a temperance house near to the dockyard gates. Enough money was raised to buy such a property and in May 1876 the first 'Sailors' Rest' was opened in Devonport. It was an immediate success and encouraged the two ladies to launch a similar project in Portsmouth in 1881. Although temperance was encouraged at lectures on the subject, and religious services were organised where participants were invited to sign the pledge, all sailors were in fact welcome to use the facilities in the Portsmouth Sailors' Rest. It offered a safe place to eat and drink away from the temptations of the streets and the many public houses, a bed for the night if required, baths and recreational activities. Between them, both Agnes and Sophia continued to serve as superintendents of the homes until their deaths. Agnes died in 1918 shortly after she was appointed a Dame Commander of the Order of the British Empire (DBE). Sophia was created a DBE in 1920. She died in 1929. Both women were given full ceremonial naval funerals. Queen Victoria endowed a cabin in the Sailors' rest in Devonport in 1895 and at the same time gave permission for the institution to be known henceforward as the Royal Sailors' Rest.

The 'Soldiers' Friend' was Miss Sarah Robinson. Like Agnes Weston, she was inspired to become a devout Christian by a sermon she heard delivered in Chiddingly Church, near Lewes in East Sussex in August 1851 by the Reverend James Vidal. At the time she was still at school in Brighton. Also, again like Agnes Weston and Sophia Wintz, she became convinced that dependency on alcohol contributed significantly to the woes of the poor among whom she initially worked. Ill-health forced her to return to the family home in Guildford and while recuperating there her concern grew for the numbers of young soldiers in the nearby garrison at Aldershot whose social life was centred exclusively round the numerous public houses. The Aldershot Mission Institute was established in 1863. She travelled the length and breadth of the country speaking in barracks and garrison towns and in 1864 visited Portsmouth for the first time. She was also shocked by the destitution faced by soldiers and their families who were not living in barrack accommodation. Equally shocking were the difficulties she faced trying to secure support for her proposal to establish a Soldiers' Institute in Portsmouth not only from some senior officers but also from the Senior Army Chaplain, Archdeacon Wright, who was adamant that she should not give religious instruction to the men who came to the Institute. However, despite the obstacles put in her way, she raised enough money and secured sufficient support from officers well-disposed to the project to purchase and pay for the renovation of the former Fountain Hotel in the High Street in the old town of Portsmouth which had stood empty for many years. This became the base for her activities thereafter.

She still faced abuse however. Gates alludes to the problems she faced in Portsmouth in the obituary notice he wrote in *Records of the Corporation.* She died in 1921 aged 87,

> In her endeavours to start an Institute, she met with much opposition, official and otherwise, but at last made up her mind to start at the Fountain, which she made her abode on January 12th 1874. On September 10th the Institute was formally opened by General Sir James Hope Grant. But the rough element in Portsmouth did their best, or worst, to drive her from the town.

He quoted from her Journal,

> When we went into the Dockyard to meet any troopship we had to pass through a mob of land sharks and women, who cursed me for 'spoiling sport' and 'taking the bread out of other people's mouths.' Mud was often thrown into my cab, our windows were broken, door-mats cut up, disgusting anonymous letters sent, and people would bawl after soldiers in the street, asking if they were some of Miss Robinson's Lambs. On November 5th I was burnt in effigy on Southsea Common.

But nothing moved her from her purpose, said Gates, and in the course of time many who were among her bitterest opponents at the start became her most ardent admirers in the end.

The Archdeacon continued to wage an extraordinary war against Sarah even after the Institute had been opened. It is tempting to wonder whether his opposition to her holding Bible classes was due to the fact that she was a woman. Pleasingly, he was passed over in favour of a civilian clergyman when the position of Chaplain General which he might reasonably have expected – and hoped – to fill, became vacant. It certainly looks as if his unreasonable opposition to what she was doing had been noted. He left Portsmouth shortly afterwards for a post in Canada.

Another initiative, launched in 1885, harnessed the resources of more of Portsmouth's unoccupied middle-class ladies. The Borough of Portsmouth Association for Nursing the Sick Poor was set up in 1885. It was affiliated to Queen Victoria's Jubilee Institute for providing Trained Nurses for the Sick Poor in 1892 and known thereafter locally as the Victoria Nursing Association. It remained in existence, adapting to changing needs as necessary, until its role was taken over by the National Health Service (NHS) after the Second World War. Its aim was not only to provide a body of skilled nurses to care for the sick poor in their own homes, but to raise 'by all the means in its power' the standard of nursing and the social position of nurses. The bound volumes of Annual Reports can be consulted in the Local History Centre in Portsmouth Central Library. They are invaluable as a record not only of the developing organisation itself, its premises and staffing arrangements, the cases attended and their nature but also for what they say about the role women played in the management of the Association and the delivery of its aims. As with the Annual Reports of the Rescue Society here are more lists of women volunteering time and effort to charitable endeavour as Vice Presidents of the Association, and as members of the Executive Council. They included the wives of senior naval and military representatives in the town, as well as the wives of local civic and business leaders.

An analysis of the names of the women who served as Vice Presidents and Members of the Council in the Association's early years include Mrs Blake, Mrs Platt, Mrs Addison, Mrs Scott Foster, Mrs Bonham Carter, Mrs Harold Pink, Mrs Lapthorn, Lady Brickwood, Mrs Mearns Fraser, Miss Gieve, and Mrs Hellyer, all of them representatives of families prominent in civic, business and church life, several of whose members would in due course espouse the cause of women's suffrage. It is tempting to ask why they did not all do so. The whole mid-twentieth century concept of the welfare state, heralded by the introduction of the National Health Service (NHS) in 1947, was inconceivable when the Association was first established. The sick poor were totally dependent on charitable giving and what little they might be able to contribute for help in their homes, and the case histories published in successive Annual Reports are sobering accounts of conditions in far too many sick rooms. What the Association's female membership learned at their meetings about the conditions in which the 'sick poor' lived; the experience they themselves gained discussing what best to do, and the unremitting struggle to cover costs and raise sufficient funds to underwrite their activities, must surely have persuaded many of them to question the political status quo. The cases cited in the very first Annual Report are typical,

> Mrs B-------, age 26, (suffering in consequence of the ignorant treatment of an unqualified Midwife) the wife of a Soldier, having three very young children, and no relative or friend to help her. When first we opened the door of the room she lodged in, and not knowing what the case was, we thought the patient must be mad, as the room was littered with straw, coal, firewood, ashes and broken crockery, the woman was standing in her nightgown with an old shawl round her head, another on her shoulders, mittens on her hands and an 'Army Blanket' half on her and half trailing on the ground. When we asked her why she was out of bed she said there was nobody to keep the children from doing mischief

and that she had been nearly out of her mind with the noise and the baby crying so because there had been no one to wash or dress him for days but that getting out of bed made her have 'the cold shivers so badly'.

We found fresh straw had been put in the bed ticking but the end had not been sewn up, so, when we had sewn that we swept the room, took away a quantity of ashes which had accumulated in the grate. Collected out of cupboards and corners all the soiled linen and clothes we could find and made arrangements to have them washed at once. We washed and dressed the two children, one aged 3 years the other eighteen months, then washed and dressed the baby, got all the shawls etc off the patient and sponged her and having cleared up all the crockery left on the table and put them out of the children's reach, we left.

The mother recovered, as did another young mother, 'Mrs H------, aged 21', who had typhoid fever. Every morning the nurses took temperatures for the information of the patient's doctor, sponged the patient and combed her hair. They took necessary precautions against bed sores and made the bed without removing the patient. They then washed and dressed the baby which was only 7 weeks old. In the evening they took temperatures once more, undressed the baby and made it comfortable for the night and prepared its food. 'Mrs A------, aged 23', the wife of an omnibus driver, was also a young mother, suffering from 'nervous prostration', possibly what we know today as post-natal depression,

The medical attendant instructed us to go to this case as he feared it might result in lunacy if she had not more judicious nursing than an old monthly nurse which she had employed was likely to give her. We found patient over anxious, seemingly about everything, especially about her infant which was very fretful and kept in patient's room, and extremely anxious about her own condition, capricious and complaining of the unkind treatment of everyone about her. She held our hands and begged us not to leave her, as she knew we would be kind to her.

The nurses cleared a great deal of superfluous furniture from the room, and took up the carpets. They carried the baby downstairs and ordered it to be kept there, gave the patient a blanket bath, persuaded her to divest herself of the numerous blankets and shawls she wanted to wrap round herself, and persuaded her to open the window an inch to air the room. They gave strict instructions to her husband to take no notice of the patient's many complaints 'but to be kind to her', and to limit visitors to one at a time. This patient made a full recovery too.

A boy of 12 called 'F.G.' with diphtheria was not so lucky. The nurses took up the carpet and put the room 'in nursing order'. They visited three times daily and 'mopped out' his throat, twice daily they sponged him with Condy's Fluid, a disinfectant, and water, between blankets, combed his hair and took necessary precautions against bed sores. As the mother was quite worn out and there was no one else who could relieve her at night, the nurses sat up with the child one night but sadly, he died. Another case to do with a child was also cited in this first report. There is no name and indeed no personal information other than the fact that the child was 8 and suffering from typhoid fever – in a dirty and miserable room devoid of all furniture but an old table and a few chairs.

Women were honing their political skills. By the 1880s they had become the mainstays of both the Liberal and Unionist election machines. According to the *Portsmouth Times* on 26 June 1886, the Ladies of the Bruce Habitation of the Primrose League (the Honourable T.C. Bruce was a candidate) were canvassing actively on behalf of Unionist candidates during the General Election campaign that year. On 22 September 1900 the Conservative agent was appealing in the *Portsmouth Times* for ladies willing to assist with clerical work to call at the Drill Hall in Hampshire Terrace, and in its edition of 13 January

1906 the paper commented on the prominent part women were playing 'carrying on the political warfare' as one of the most notable features of the general election that year. They included members of the Primrose League, the Women's Tariff Reform League, the Women's Liberal Unionist Association, the Women's Suffrage Society [sic], the Women's Liberal Federation, the Women's Liberal Association, the Women's Co-operative Guild and the Women's Temperance Association.

The first women to be elected to public office in Portsmouth were the four ladies elected as members of the Board of Guardians in the Guardians Elections on 15 December 1894. They were Mrs E.F. Proctor, Miss McCoy, Mrs M.R. Ward and Mrs M. Byerley. Gates reported that,

> many who viewed the innovation with disfavour soon had reason to change their views, as the ladies then, and in increasing measure ever since, proved not only their ability to take part in Poor Law administration, but they brought to the task a sympathetic understanding which was not a characteristic of exclusive male government. In many ways the poor and the sick are the better for the admission of lady members.

The quality of girls' education in Portsmouth had improved immeasurably by this time. The enlightened Vicar of St Thomas's Church in the old town of Portsmouth, Canon Edward Grant, who had turned round the fortunes of the moribund Grammar School in the 1870s, now turned his mind to provision for girls. There were a number of private schools for the 'neat and trim' girls in Southsea. Several had been in existence since the middle of the century such as 'The Hermitage' in Grove Road South which took boarding and day pupils chiefly from the Services but Grant felt that many of these schools were snobbish and unsatisfactory academically. 'Upper Mount' in Clarendon Road 'for the daughters of Gentlemen' was a case in point. He got in touch with a group of business and professional men, presumably with daughters of their own, and they asked the

# "Upper Mount,"

16, Clarendon Road, Southsea. .   .   .

## Boarding and
## Day School

For the Daughters of Gentlemen. .   .   .

LARGE AND EFFICIENT STAFF.

Good Games Field.                           Preparatory Class.

*For Prospectus and Particulars, address—*

MISS8DAVIES, Registered Teacher, Board of Education.

MISS VINES, L.R.A.M., L·L.C.M.

*Advertisement for Upper Mount School from* The Portsmouth and Southsea Guide, *1920. Author's Collection.*

Girls' Public Day School Company to follow up their Brighton School by founding a similar school in Portsmouth. Shares were purchased in the company and in 1882 the school opened in Marlborough House, Osborne Road, Southsea. The school's academic credentials were firmly established when, not long after the school opened, Miss Lily Flowers won a mathematics scholarship at Newnham College, Cambridge.

By 1910 Portsmouth High School headed the list of girls' schools in the *Official Guide* to the town. Their red-brick purpose-built premises, now on the corner of Kent Road and Sussex Road and incorporating Owen's Swiss Cottage, could accommodate 300 girls. There was a Preparatory Department for boys and girls, and a boarding house nearby for pupils who came from a distance. Girls were prepared for the examinations of the Joint Board of Oxford and Cambridge, for London Matriculation, and for University Scholarships. Recent successes, their advertisement recorded, included a Clothworkers' Scholarship of £60 for three years at Girton College, Cambridge; a Classical and English Scholarship of £50 for three years at Royal Holloway College, and a Licentiateship of the Royal Academy of Music. The *Guide* also lists, after the High School and before the schools for daughters of 'gentlemen only', the 'Portsmouth Council' Girls Secondary School in Fawcett Road which had opened three years before in 1907. It had accommodation for 400 girls. The curriculum included Latin, French, Botany and Science. In short, according to the *Guide*, should a family be considering moving to Portsmouth, 'they need not be deterred by any fear of sacrificing their ... daughters' educational prospects.'

Another catalyst for change must have been the opening of a free public library with some 2,000 books in April 1883; a proclamation, as was said at the opening of Birmingham's Free Library in 1866, 'that a town ... exists for moral and intellectual purposes' as well as cleaning and lighting the streets, and mending pot holes. The new facility was located in a building at the corner of Commercial Road and Park Road which had been occupied formerly by the Commanding Officer of the Royal

Artillery and was the precursor of Portsmouth's present Central Library and its network of branch libraries. Similar sentiments must have underpinned the support the borough council gave to the introduction of university extension lectures in Portsmouth in 1886. According to Edwin Welch in his *Portsmouth Record Series* Volume 5, 'Records of University Adult Education 1886–1939', there was a constantly increasing demand for further education in late Victorian England. Women were as keen as men to continue their education and,

> when Cambridge began to offer courses of lectures followed by examinations in such cities as Portsmouth the impact was spectacular. Large numbers of students enrolled and it seemed that a course on any subject would be a success, simply for want of any alternative source of instruction. The early university extension student attended all the courses that were offered and did not select as a later student would.

Once again it was the indefatigable Canon Grant who played a significant role in developing a Cambridge Extension Scheme for Portsmouth. A committee was formed at a meeting held on 22 January 1886 in St Thomas's Vicarage. An Honorary Secretary of a provisional committee was appointed and there was discussion on a possible initial course. The choice was between 'Astronomy' and 'Literature of the Elizabethan Age'. Astronomy was clearly agreed and the course began shortly afterwards. While almost 150 people attended the lectures, there is no information on whether they were male or female but record-keeping did improve. A course began in the Guildhall at 8.00 p.m. on 27 January in the Lent Term 1888 on 'The chemistry of animal and vegetable life', and the names of the participants are cited for the first time. Of the forty-five who received certificates following the end of term examination, twenty-five were women, two of whom were recommended for special distinction: Emily Cogill and Mildred Twiss.

Emily also secured a special distinction in the Michaelmas Term 1888 examinations at the end of a course on 'Matter, motion and force'. Of the 27 candidates who sat that examination, there were six special distinctions, and half of these were women. Initially, the courses were financed solely from students' fees, but after 1888 the Borough Council was empowered to make grants for technical education. The word 'technical' was interpreted generously and a broad range of courses was delivered on the sciences and humanities. At the end of the Michaelmas Term 1889 course on 'The French Revolution' Emily Cogill achieved another special distinction and in May 1890 was awarded the Vice-Chancellor's certificate. A Review of the work of the Portsmouth University Extension Centre was carried out in 1899. The total attendance at lectures since 1886 was over 27,000, and at classes over 20,000 which averaged eighty-three people at each evening and thirty-eight at each afternoon lecture, and sixty at each evening and twenty-seven at each afternoon class. Overall, 739 individuals submitted written work during the courses and 582 people sat examinations. Of these last, 536 passed and 126 received special distinctions. The organisers were proud of their efforts and noted in their report that while this sort of information was easy to tabulate,

> there are other results which cannot be so expressed, and which show the educational benefit to the town derived from having these courses of lectures. The amount of good work done in this way it is impossible to estimate.

While no work has been done on the subject, from what evidence there is in Welch's book, it does look as if a good half, if not more, of the overall participants in these early university extension classes were young middle- and upper-middle class women. Emily Cogill lived in Merton Road in the heart of the business and professional enclave of Owen's Southsea. Some of the names of attendees, where they exist, are still familiar in local business circles (e.g. the Miss Lapthorns) and it is significant that course organisers expressed concern in occasional reports that the cost of courses might discourage 'artisan' subscribers. They were also concerned that Portsmouth was a garrison town, and largely made up of what the 1899 Review called the 'the naval and military element' i.e. families who were settled there only briefly. 'Such a class of people', the writer maintained,

> never remain long in one town, and thus have no interest in taking part in any of its educational movements; for, granting that they have an inclination so to do, no sooner have they taken up the work than they are removed to another town. As for the civil element, a large majority have employment in the Dockyard, and after their duties there do not seem to interest themselves much in higher education.

Portsmouth's young women were interested however. They were not deterred by the preponderance of science subjects and signed up in large numbers for most subjects but particularly for courses on 'Shakespeare's English historical plays' and 'Shakespeare's comedies and tragedies', also 'Plants: their structure and their habits'. Two terms of lectures on architecture proved equally popular. More further education opportunities for young women from a broader range of local society came with the opening of a Technical College in disused municipal offices in Arundel Street in 1893. Working as a governess or teaching in a school had always been an option for an intelligent girl with some education but no money. Among the courses established in the new college was one in a separate pupil-teacher centre for trainee teachers, the majority of whom were young women. The somewhat makeshift facilities in Arundel Street were replaced in 1907 by the Municipal College, built behind the Town Hall on what had been known as the Mayor's Lawn. It was designed to accommodate a number of Science, Technical and Arts courses, the Municipal School of Art which had been established in Pembroke Road in 1871, the town library and the Pupil Teacher centre. However, a decision was made in August 1907 shortly before the new Municipal College opened in October to establish a Day Training College for Women. Under successive principals from 1907 until 1976 when it ceased to exist in its own right the training college delivered a highly-regarded liberal education for young trainee teachers which Professor Sadler considered so vital in his Report into the State of Technical Education in Liverpool in 1904. A liberal education, he maintained, 'was necessary for entrance to all professions' and 'is ... the foundation upon which the technical training of the teacher ... is built up'.

The first intake in 1907 to the Day Training College was heavily over-subscribed. There were 250 applications for 90 places, a good half of whom were from local pupil teachers, qualified to enter a training college but unable to find places, whose protests to the council earlier in the year had undoubtedly been a factor in the decision to establish a training college in Portsmouth. Remembering college life in those early days, members of the first intake recalled many

*The Municipal College, c.1907. Author's Collection.*

years later 'hard work intermingled with play and happy social discourse, and – with particular pleasure – the sheer fun of living together in hostels in central Southsea and the 'dark, delightful secrets that were enjoyed'. They acknowledged too what they owed to their tutors and lecturers, and one girl wrote that 'we also owe something, through interchange of ideas and opinions to our fellow-students'. And in that interchange of ideas and opinions the subject of women's suffrage was roundly discussed. Mrs F.K. Robins (Miss Bates 1910–12) recalled that the women's suffrage movement was very active,

> and we all felt it to be a thrilling adventure when a real, live suffragette came and addressed us one afternoon in the Hostel Common Room. Her name I cannot remember, but she was a quite delightful personality and not the ogress that some of us rather expected to see. Battles royal sometimes occurred in our hostel when political matters came up for discussion. Lloyd George being one of the great storm centres.

## CHAPTER FIVE

# Suffragists and Suffragettes

✳✳✳

The fight for the vote in Portsmouth was led not by Mrs Emmeline Pankhurst's militant organisation, the Women's Social and Political Union (WSPU), whose members were known as the suffragettes, a word coined by the *Daily Mail*; the fight in the town was led by the local branch of the non-militants, the suffragists, members of Mrs Millicent Fawcett's National Union of Women's Suffrage Societies (NUWSS). Sources are limited. No official records survive locally of the different branches of the suffrage societies, and all that survives in the official records of the NUWSS and WSPU in the Women's Library at the London School of Economics is a testimonial presented to Miss Norah O'Shea who was the Secretary of the local branch of the NUWSS.

A small collection of books survives in the Portsmouth History Centre. It looks as if it was a small lending library belonging to local suffragists. The titles reflect the issues concerning their readers: *A New Conscience and an Ancient Evil,* and *The Spirit of Youth and the City Streets*, both by Jane Adams; *Sweated Industry and the Minimum Wage* by Clementina Black; *The Status of Women under the English Law* by A. Beatrice Wallis Chapman and Mary Wallis Chapman; *Thoughts on Some Questions relating to Women 1860–1908* by Emily Davies; *The Emancipation of English Women* by W. Lyon Blease; *Women and Labour* by Olive Schreiner and *The Soul Market* by Olive Christian Malvery. There are also copies of Sylvia Pankhurst's collection of verse, *Writ on Cold Slate,* and several prints of a prison cell inscribed:

'You have made of your prisons a temple of honour'. Scribbled inside a number of the books is a note from Norah O'Shea urging the reader to return them when read.

There is also Harriet Blessley's manuscript account of the great march to London by a contingent of local non-militants in July 1913, and Lancelot Surry's typescript recollections of his mother's activities as a member of the WSPU but the main source of information about the fight for the vote in Portsmouth is local newspapers. The suffrage campaign was good copy and through the pages of the *Portsmouth Evening News,* the *Hampshire Telegraph* and the *Portsmouth Times,* it is possible to reconstruct a narrative. Qualified, rate-paying spinsters had in fact been able to vote in borough elections since 1869 and in county council elections since 1888, and some 2,705 Portsmouth women were entitled thus to vote. These franchises were extended to married women in 1894, although it was noted in 1911 by the Mayor, Mr Tom Scott Foster, that very few of them were taking the trouble to vote which is surprising because it is clear in the columns of the local newspapers that women's suffrage was a big issue locally.

Possibly it was a generational matter. The strength of local opinion can be gauged in the report in the *Hampshire Telegraph* of a meeting organised by the NUWSS in Cosham in January 1909. The speaker, Mrs Harrison Bell, took as her subject 'The Industrial Position of Women' and pointed to the many ways in which the granting of the franchise to women would affect their position in the industrial world. They could negotiate for better and fairer wages. They could influence legislation affecting children and the home, housing, the medical inspection and feeding of children. They could also better protect the interests of poorer classes of women. At a meeting of the Portsmouth branch of the WSPU twelve months later very similar views were being expressed by a speaker from London, a Miss Carey. 'It was totally unjust,' she said, that women had to stand helplessly by,

> when there were so many important questions before the country, a large proportion of which materially affected

women's interests. A wealthy woman who owned houses and land, who employed servants and work people was yet debarred, merely because of her sex, from having any say by way of a vote, in the political questions which were so vital to her interests.

Frederick Pethick-Lawrence raised the debate onto an even more elevated plane when he spoke at a meeting organised by the WSPU in Portsmouth in late 1911. At the time he was joint-editor with his wife, Emmeline, of *Votes for Women,* the official organ of the WSPU,

> It is fighting for the dignity of your souls; it is fighting for the right to have an opinion which is not a subordinate opinion that is fighting for the right to stand on a footing of equality with the other half of the human race.

He was received rapturously.

All the national suffrage societies were represented in Portsmouth and its immediate neighbourhood. Lancelot Surry maintained that Portsmouth was an important provincial centre. The NUWSS was certainly the most active organisation if column inches in local newspapers are any indication of the scale of their operation. There were branches in Portsmouth, Gosport, Petersfield and Chichester. The WSPU followed closely behind. Other organisations active locally in the cause of women's suffrage included the Women's Liberal Association, the Conservative and Unionist Women's Franchise Association, the British Women's Temperance Society, the Independent Labour Party, the Women's Labour League, the Portsmouth Midwives Association, the Women's Co-operative Guild, the National Union of Women Workers, the National Union of Teachers, the Women's Freedom League and the Church League for Women's Suffrage.

There were also branches of the Women's National Anti-Suffrage League in the Portsmouth area. The League was formed in July 1908 in response to the challenge thrown down to the suffragists by the Prime Minister, Herbert Asquith, to show that they had a majority of British women behind them. The League's leader in the South of England was Miss Mary Anne Dickens, granddaughter of the novelist Charles Dickens, born in Mile End, Portsmouth, in 1812. The inaugural meeting of the Portsmouth branch was held at the Sandringham Hall in Southsea on 9 February 1909. Miss Dickens expounded the League's philosophy in an interview with the *Hampshire Telegraph* the day before the meeting. She dismissed the notion that enfranchisement would raise women's wages. She said such a claim was unproven and maintained that Parliament could be trusted to legislate on behalf of women and children. 'We would leave to men', she said,

> the political rule and maintenance of the vast and complex Empire which men have created, while we women strengthen our influence in the great field of local government.

At the inaugural meeting itself she urged the audience to support the league. Their indifference might lead to the vote being granted. The *Hampshire Telegraph* published the League's manifesto. It prompted a swift and crisp response from Norah O'Shea, and the chairman of the local branch of the NUWSS, Mrs Julia Hawksley, challenged Miss Dickens to take part in an open debate on the subject of women's suffrage. The Anti-Suffragists declined the invitation.

By an extraordinary coincidence, and unknown to Miss Dickens, Ellen Ternan, the impecunious widow of the Reverend George Wharton Robinson was living now in Southsea. She and her two sisters had been child actresses. She had met Dickens in 1857 when he was 45 and she was only 18. She was Dickens's secret mistress for the best part of the decade between 1860 and 1870 when he died. They probably had at least one child and possibly more, but there is no evidence to suggest that these children survived. Dickens did provide for her in his will. Ellen was bright with a facility for languages and six years after Dickens' death she married Wharton Robinson, an Oxford graduate. They had two children in due course and ran a school together in Margate. They settled in Southsea c.1906 where Ellen's sisters had been living for a little while, and Ellen coached young army officers who needed to acquire some skill speaking French, Italian and German. When George died in 1910 Ellen moved in with her surviving, widowed, sister, Mrs Fanny Trollope, sister-in-law of the author Anthony Trollope, to maximise their limited resources; they wrote plays to amuse themselves, possibly in the hope that they might produce something which would attract the attention of a publisher. They also took a keen interest in politics. Early in 1911 they joined the Anti-Suffrage League and, although by now in their seventies, they went to hear Miss Dickens address an anti-suffrage meeting in Southsea.

The members of both the NUWSS and the WSPU seem to have been recruited almost exclusively from the ranks of the middle classes in local society. The NUWSS attracted the 'neat, trim' daughters and the wives of men of independent means, the professions, business and the Services. Norah O'Shea and her sister Margaret, five years her senior, are good examples. Born in 1865, Norah was in her early forties when the local branch of the NUWSS was established in Portsmouth c.1908–9. She and Margaret came from a long and distinguished line of naval men who had married very sensibly into Portsmouth's wealthy aldermanic ranks in the late eighteenth and early nineteenth centuries.

They were the great-granddaughters of baronet Sir Roger Curtis, Lord Howe's flag captain at the Glorious First of June in 1794, the first naval battle between the British and the French during the Revolutionary Wars. Sir Roger was also Commander-in-Chief at Portsmouth 1809–12. His eldest son (another Roger), a post captain, had predeceased him in 1812 so the baronetcy passed on his death in 1816 to his second son, Lucius, the girls' grandfather, one of Nelson's protégés. Lucius in turn became an Admiral of the Fleet, a Companion of the Order of the Bath and a Deputy Lieutenant of Hampshire. He was living at East Cosham Cottage in 1861 on the night of the census with his

*The Dickens Birthplace. It was purchased by the Town Council in 1903 to display books and memorabilia associated with Dickens but the Ternan sisters never divulged any connection with him in the years they lived in the town, n.d. Author's Collection.*

unmarried, youngest daughter, Frances. His married, eldest daughter, Mary, her husband and children were also living there with the children's governess, a cook and four maids.

Sir Lucius died in 1869 and in 1871 Frances, now on her own and described as an 'annuitant' and the head of the household in the census that year, is living at East Cosham Cottage with four servants. She died in early 1891 and Margaret and Norah's mother, Elizabeth O'Shea, Sir Lucius's second daughter (he had three), is listed in the census that year as the head of the household. She is described as a widow and 'living on own means'. Two of her daughters, Margaret and Norah, are living with her as well as a cook, a parlour maid and a house maid. Elizabeth died in 1908 and it looks as if her daughters then inherited the property.

A few years ago descendants of their domestic staff suggested that Margaret and Norah were the daughters of Charles Stewart Parnell, the charismatic Irish MP and leader of the Irish Parliamentary Party at Westminster, and his mistress, Mrs Katharine O'Shea (née Wood), known as 'Kitty' in the popular press because at that time 'kitty' was slang for a prostitute. In her own family Katharine was known as Katie. When the scandal of Parnell's liaison with Mrs O'Shea broke in 1890 public opinion was shocked and outraged, particularly non-conformist opinion. Parnell's career was finished as were his hopes of securing Home Rule for Ireland through Gladstone and the Liberals.

Margaret and Norah could not have been the daughters of Parnell and Mrs Katharine O'Shea though. The birth dates of the different girls in the two families do not tie up. Miss Katharine Wood married first a Captain William O'Shea in 1867, a Catholic nationalist MP for County Clare from whom she separated in 1875. She had three children by O'Shea: Gerard William Henry in 1870, Mary Norah Kathleen (Norah) in 1873 and Anna Maria del Carmen (Carmen) in 1874. Then, after 1880 when she first met Parnell, she had three children by him in quick succession: Claude Sophie (who died shortly after birth) early in 1882, Claire Gabrielle Antoinette Marcia born in

1883 and Frances Katharine Flavia (Katie) born in 1884. The fact that one of the children by her marriage to Captain William O'Shea was called Norah must have fuelled the speculation in Portsmouth years later about their Norah's parentage.

The fact that Sir Lucius Curtis's daughter, Elizabeth, also married an army officer called O'Shea probably added to the confusion. She is described as the widow of Major Rodney Fane O'Shea of the Twentieth Foot (Regiment) in the Christ Church Portsdown Burial Register when she was buried in that churchyard on 11 August 1908. (The Twentieth were the East Devon's.) Rodney and Elizabeth were living in Millbrook, Southampton in 1861. He was 38 and Elizabeth was 36. They had three small daughters at this point, the youngest being Margaret, aged 1. At the time of the 1881 census, Elizabeth is living in Moss Side, Lancashire. She is described as the Head of the Household but married and not widowed. Presumably Rodney was stationed elsewhere. Six children were listed in 1881: Frances Eliza (24), Margaret Mary Elizabeth (21), Rodney Lacy Roberts (19), Henry (17), Norah (16) and Clara (14). This Norah, the daughter of Rodney and Elizabeth, was therefore born in 1865. She died in 1953 aged 88. By 1891 the widowed Elizabeth, Margaret and Norah are living in East Cosham Cottage. After 1908 and their mother's death, they lived there until the late 1920s. They are listed in the property in 1925 but they are not there in 1929. The house had been acquired by this time by Dr James Bell, physician and surgeon, and the Cosham MOH.

According to anecdotal evidence, East Cosham Cottage was the unofficial headquarters of the Portsmouth Branch of the NUWSS from c.1907 until c.1913. The house had been in the family since c.1816. Sir Roger Curtis had owned and lived at Gatcombe House at Hilsea. It had been part of the dowry of his wife, Sarah, the daughter of Matteate Brady (a curious Christian name; possibly a contraction of the name Matthew and his mother's maiden surname of Teate). Sir Roger married Sarah in 1744 and when he died in 1816 Gatcombe House and the surrounding lands were compulsorily purchased by the War Office. At this point his son, now Sir Lucius, purchased East

Cosham Cottage on the mainland, a few miles to the north of Gatcombe, on the northern side of the Havant Road immediately facing Park Lane. It was certainly not an agricultural cottage. There were ten adults and four children living there in 1861, and descendants of staff who worked there for the two sisters in the late nineteenth and early twentieth centuries recalled that there was a lot of fine furniture and paintings, and the lawns abutting the property hosted many charitable and fundraising activities for the suffragist cause.

There was also a coachman called Charles Andrews who drove the brougham in a maroon livery. A brougham was a light, four-wheeled horse-drawn carriage which had an enclosed body with two doors. It was like the rear half of a coach and seated two, but there may have been a pair of fold-away seats given how large the household was on occasions. A box seat in the front accommodated the driver and another passenger or a footman. The carriage also had a glazed front window so that the passengers could see forward. It was a manoeuvrable vehicle, capable of turning sharply. It was still in regular use before the First World War and there are stories of Norah summoning Charles as late as 11.00 p.m. to take a letter down to the Head Post Office in Commercial Road opposite the Town Station to catch the night mail for London.

Both the O'Shea sisters were suffrage activists. According to an article in the *Evening News* on 7 May 1963, Norah was 'the red-haired rebel' and Margaret was 'dark, quiet and stately'. It was Margaret though who composed the words of their suffrage song, inspired surely by the plight of Portsmouth women working making shirts or in local stay factories,

> Forward, brave and dauntless
> Daughters of this earth,
> Let your dormant talents
> Spring to glorious birth.
>
> Children, toiling sisters,
> Cry, and never rest;

## VOTES FOR WOMEN.

### SUFFRAGISTS AT COSHAM.

### PRETTY GARDEN FETE.

There was a pretty scene at the Cottage, Cosham, on Wednesday afternoon, when a garden fete was held in aid of the fund of the Portsmouth branch of the National Union of Women's Suffrage. On the prettily-kept lawns stalls were arranged, from which articles of a dainty and useful nature were dispensed. Mrs. Lapthorn, Miss Row-, and Mrs. Piggott had charge of the fancy stall, and Mrs. Hawksley superintended a pottery stall, while there was a refreshment stall under the charge of Mrs. Harris, Mrs. Croaker, and Mrs. Whittick.

Miss N. O'Shea introduced Lady Grove to those assembled, and remarked that they were most grateful to her Ladyship for coming down from London to open the fete and speak.

Lady Grove at once referred to the attitude and actions of the militant section of the women suffragists. She did not see that any object was to be gained by the tactics which were employed by that section, but was of opinion that they were putting ''eir cause back in a way that nothing else could do. When the Women's Suffrage movement was begun those tactics drew attention to a subject that was little considered by the people, but conduct such as they had witnessed on Tuesday night could do no possible good, as the light of the world was now shining on those who were taking part in the movement. They demanded admission to the House of Commons to see a Minister who they knew perfectly well was not there, and when they were told that the Minister could not see them, she (the speaker) regretted to see that a lady leader so far forgot herself as to use violence to a police officer who was simply doing his duty. How could they convince people that they were reasonable when such violent and virulent conduct as this was possible? Lady Grove proceeded to urge the justice of the claim for women's suffrage. The whole of the suffrage societies were agreed upon the request that the vote should be extended to women upon the same terms as it was, or might be, granted to men. Responsibility, she contended, was a great asset in the development of character. It was character that would save the English people, and not ships and guns; and if this was to be imprinted in the minds of the children of the nation, it should be done at birth. The sense of responsibility, therefore, should not be confined to men, as in cases of emergency and necessity women had shown, and would continue to show, that they were to be relied upon as well. (Applause.)

A vote of thanks was accorded to Lady Grove for speaking, and to the Misses O'Shea for the arrangement of the fete.

During the remainder of the afternoon and evening some very interesting entertainments were given in the house and garden. Morris and national dances by Miss Deal's troupe, the members of which were charmingly attired in costumes of purple, blue and gold, were especially attractive. Entertainments, arranged by Miss Meyer, were given in the house, and included recitations by Mrs. Markham Phillips, and Spanish songs by Mrs. Hayward, and a conjuring entertainment by Mr. R. Kay, and a programme by Miss Jones' band were presented in the open air. As a finale there were sports in the field.

Answer! We shall help you
Coming to our best.

Forward, fighting evils,
Deborahs, awake!
Up and help your sisters
Victims at life's stake.

Besides their suffrage work, the sisters had dogs, Norah was certainly vegetarian and between them they were particularly keen on homeopathic medicine. A recent historian of Cosham, Anida Rayfield, touched on the sisters in her booklet *Discovering Cosham*,

They were well-known in the village as 'doers of good works'... Norah however achieved some national fame as an ardent worker for women's rights; she organized open-air meetings and raised funds for the cause. The sisters are still remembered by people living in Cosham, and there is general agreement that they died penniless having given their money away.

This was not entirely right. Their former servants allege that the women lost their income after the First World War because their money was invested principally in the German Krupp family's steel, artillery and armaments business. This is more than possible because after the war the firm was forced to give up arms manufacturing.

*Cutting from the* Portsmouth Times *reporting on a garden fête held at The Cottage, Cosham, 1 July 1909. Portsmouth History Centre.*

It tried to redirect its efforts into consumer products but operated at a loss for many years. According to their staff, the sisters began growing flowers in their gardens and glasshouses to supplement their income from c.1920, for sale on their own premises and to local wholesalers. East Cosham Cottage and probably the property within its curtilage, inhabited by the coachman, Charles Andrews, are numbered by this time in directories as Nos. 51 and 53, Havant Road, and they are described variously as 'Florists', 'The Nurseries' and 'The Cottage'. But this was clearly not the answer to the sisters' financial problems. They had to downsize.

They were living in 'The Cottage' in 1925 but must have moved soon afterwards to rooms in Southsea for Margaret died in 1927 and was brought from 30, Alhambra Road, Southsea to be buried on 23 November in Milton Cemetery. Alhambra Road is a street of substantial terraced houses running north from South Parade and South Parade Pier, behind a number of Owen villas and terraces overlooking the sea. Presumably Norah could not afford to stay there on her own for she is listed living in rooms in a more modest semi-detached villa at 14, Kenilworth Road, Southsea in 1929. Later the same year she is living in a small terraced house at 13, Edgeware Road, Milton. She is there until 1941. She is not there at the end of the war. She died though in 1953 at the age of 88 and was brought from 21, Weston Avenue, Milton, another small terraced property not that far from Edgeware Road and behind St James's Church, Milton, to be buried in Milton Cemetery. There is no memorial to the sisters.

Their plight was not unusual. They are typical of many single women at this time from similar middle-class backgrounds who did not marry for any number of different reasons, had received no higher education, or been trained in any profession or calling which might have enabled them to earn a decent living – and were entirely dependent for their income on the yield from investments. If businesses failed or leases fell in, they were destitute. The sisters and their fellow-suffragists fought valiantly to secure the vote to better protect poorer women and their families at home and at work. It is truly ironic that the sisters who worked so hard for the women's suffrage movement should, at the end of their own lives, be victims of a system still weighted so heavily in favour of men.

Of the other members of the Portsmouth branch of the NUWSS, Mrs Lapthorn, the president, was well-connected in local legal and professional circles, and Mrs Hawksley was the wife of the Reverend W. Hawksley, the vicar of All Saints, Landport. NUWSS meetings also attracted the wives and daughters of local minor gentry. The Conservative and Unionist Women's Franchise Association attracted a similar cross-section of local society as the list of guests at a garden party in 1912 at 'Oaklands' in Stakes Hill shows: Brigadier-General Sir Robert and Lady Colleton, Mrs and Miss Bashford of Soberton Towers, Mrs Hoare of Purbrook Park, Miss Deverell, Mrs Thistlethwayte, and Mr and Mrs Hulbert of Stakes Hill Lodge. The speaker was Lady Selborne on the subject of the Reform Bill then before the House of Commons which proposed giving universal male suffrage. Conservative suffragists proposed amending the bill with a clause giving the vote to those women who already possessed the municipal qualification. Lady Selborne begged the meeting to urge the local MP, Mr Arthur Lee, to support the amendment. She was a doughty and indefatigable speaker on behalf of the suffrage cause not only locally but nationally. The wife of the Earl of Selborne, she was President of the Conservative and Unionist Women's Franchise Association, and a daughter of the Marquis of Salisbury, the former Conservative prime minister. She and her husband lived at Blackmoor, between Selborne and Liss, just north of Petersfield.

'The statesmanlike course for the Conservatives to adopt', she pronounced at Oaklands, 'was to support and carry into law a moderate measure while they could yet do it'. She continued presciently,

> The opposition would very soon be passed, if it had not already passed. The Conservatives had always been

the 'stupid' party – (laughter) – and she supposed they would go on being the stupid party, by refusing to do things which would really help their cause until it was too late.... This would be their last chance, and if they did not take it a very much wider measure would be passed as soon as the Labour party had eaten up the Liberals, which would not be very long. Let them make no mistake, the Labour party were going to be the future Liberal party.

As for the local branch of the WSPU, it is probably best described as being not quite so 'genteel' as the local branches of the NUWSS. It attracted the 'neat, trim' girls who were frustrated by the failure of the NUWSS to make any progress but it also attracted the young women who were beginning to make tentative inroads into business and professional life such as the young lady sanitary inspector noted by young Lancelot Surry,

> The organiser was a tall young woman, of quiet, resolute bearing. She was supposed to have been a sanitary inspector before she became an advocate of the WSPU. Her photograph used to hang in our home. It bore an inscription to the effect that for the sake of women's rights she had undergone imprisonment in Holloway Gaol. I suppose she was regarded as a martyr. If so, I never met a more cold-blooded martyr.

The local WSPU also seems to have attracted the wives and daughters of local tradesmen. There was a little woman with 'fishy eyes', according to Lancelot, who spoke very meekly to organisers, and turned out to be a dealer who did very well out of fundraising rummage sales. Another branch member he describes was a stout, red-faced woman 'plainly in the movement to help along her husband's business'. He was a money-lender.

It is clear from local newspaper reports that WSPU meetings were livelier than those of the NUWSS. Speakers such as Miss Catherine Margesson, daughter of Sir Mortimer and Lady

Margesson, a Newnham College, Cambridge graduate, and the WSPU organizer in Reading, spoke enthusiastically about the use of agitation and insisted in front of crowds in Portsmouth's Town Hall Square in July 1913 that it was their only weapon. It was the government's fault. For sixty years they had tried legal and constitutional methods to secure the vote which women needed,

> to protect their position in the industrial world, to better their conditions and to give power to their trade unions to enforce their claims on the members of Parliament.

The president of the Portsmouth branch of the WSPU was Mrs Cather and the secretary was a Miss Peacock. The sanitary inspector so disliked by Lancelot Surry may have been Miss Charlotte Marsh. She is listed in the Portsmouth MOH's Annual Reports as a member of his staff. She seems to have been the first female appointment. The WSPU also had powerful clerical allies. One of the staunchest was the Reverend G.W. Thompson, minister of the Unitarian Church in the High Street, Portsmouth. His support for women's suffrage brought him a large congregation of women. He was also an active speaker on the subject in Portsmouth and the surrounding area. From the other end of the local religious spectrum came the Reverend E. Bruce Cornford of St Matthew's Church Southsea. A ritualist, he still wanted justice and fairness for women and supported militancy if it would help them achieve their aims.

The women's suffrage movement in Portsmouth was never a working-class movement. While the members of the local branches of both the NUWSS and the WSPU were anxious to improve the lot of women working in the dress trades there is no evidence to suggest that women in the stay factories, for example, were involved personally in the fight. They were too busy scraping a living. It should also be noted that while the story of the fight for the vote nationally becomes the story of the WSPU from 1906 as it abandoned legal and constitutional tactics for militancy, the history of the fight for the vote in the regions may be rather different. Local branches of the NUWSS which continued to espouse constitutional tactics to the end were more active in the Portsmouth area than the national picture would seem to indicate.

The *Hampshire Telegraph* followed the whole debate with considerable interest. It deplored the 'unwomanly tactics' of Mrs Drummond and her four companions who chained themselves to the railings of No. 10, Downing Street in January 1908 but conceded that the women had a point as they had been promised redress,

> These women are in deadly earnest, or they would not submit to the ridicule, opprobrium and imprisonment to which their agitation leads, and if the Government wish to put an end to such pitiable exhibitions as that of Downing Street yesterday they should give an undertaking that the just demands of the women shall be met.

The paper also published details about the conditions the women had to endure in prison particularly the quality of the food and suggested that ridicule for the women was changing to sympathy 'due as much to the harsh treatment to which they are subjected as to the courageous manner in which they are taking their punishment'. However, the local branches of the Women's Liberal Association and the NUWSS both disassociated themselves from such tactics and continued to commit themselves to conventional – and constitutional – forms of protest.

A deputation led by Norah O'Shea waited upon the junior member for the borough, Mr T.A. Bramsdon, at his home in Elm Grove in February 1908 and urged him to be present in the House of Commons on the day Mr H.Y. Stanger's Private Member's Bill came up for its second reading. Norah was very keen that their MP should understand that they were not militant. He was pleased to hear this but the *Hampshire Telegraph* pointed out that the militants' tactics were attracting more attention from the government than all the resolutions of 'the more sedate members of the suffrage societies. It would be another twelve months before the paper questioned the wisdom of militancy. In the meantime the Portsmouth branch of the NUWSS continued to campaign for Stanger's Bill – and the inaugural meeting was called of the Portsmouth branch of the Women's Labour League on the subject of sweating and the feasibility of setting up a trade union among Portsmouth's women corset workers.

Two key demonstrations took place in London during the summer months of 1908 in the hope that such strong – non-militant – displays of female solidarity might help the cause as Stanger's Bill made its journey through parliament. The NUWSS organised a procession in which 15,000 men and women took part. They marched with banners aloft from the Embankment to the Albert Hall. Members of the Portsmouth branch of the NUWSS carried a banner emblazoned with Nelson's signal: 'Engage the enemy more closely'. Norah informed the *Hampshire Telegraph* reporter that it was one of their proudest moments,

> our banner was the first one unfurled. We met at Northumberland-avenue, and with the assistance of civilians and helpers, we raised our banner first. Of course we expected a lot of bitter things said to and about us, and feared that things would be thrown at us but they were not. Of course we had a lot of good-natured chaff, but the sympathy of the men in the street was admirable…'Good old Pompey', 'Well done, Portsmouth'. Such were the exclamations heard on all sides, and one Marine even saluted the banner.

A sailor they met wanted to carry it but he was not allowed to do so. The *Hampshire Telegraph* was very impressed with the day's proceedings. The women are demanding rights, it said, which should not be withheld for much longer.

The WSPU's leaders were present but they were planning their own demonstration. The 'Great Shout' took place in Hyde

Park in June. There had never been a demonstration like it. *The Times* reckoned that half a million individuals, mainly women, took part. Some thirty special trains brought demonstrators into London, many sporting the new WSPU colours of purple, white and green devised by Emmeline Pethick-Lawrence to distinguish the membership from the NUWSS whose colours were red, white and green. A special train ran from Portsmouth to London Waterloo stopping only once at Petersfield. There were between five and six hundred people on board. At Waterloo Station the Portsmouth contingent met up with the passengers on the Southampton special, and led by a London and South Western Railway band, they all marched together to Trafalgar Square. Besides local members of the WSPU there were also representatives of the Women's Labour League and the Labour Party. From Trafalgar Square the marchers made their way to Hyde Park. There was a choice of some twenty platforms and the Portsmouth women made their way to Mrs Pethick-Lawrence's platform to hear her speak. A resolution was agreed and sent by special messenger to the Prime Minister, Herbert Asquith. He ignored it and the WSPU resumed militant tactics at the end of June 1908.

The violence was not replicated in Portsmouth. In fact the local branch of the NUWSS deplored the violence and devoted its energies to promoting a series of drawing room meetings across the area as part of their educational programme. The climax of their activities was a mass meeting held on 11 November in the Town Hall. It was described in the papers as one of the largest political or semi-political meetings which had ever taken place there. All political persuasions were present and it was standing room only. The banners which had been carried in London in the summer were draped round the walls. The platform party included Mrs Godfrey Baring, wife of the MP for the Isle of Wight who presided, Lady Frances Balfour, daughter of the eighth duke of Argyle and sister-in-law of Mr A.J. Balfour, Mr and Mrs Bramsdon, Colonel A.R. Holbrook, proprietor and publisher of the *Portsmouth Times*, NUWSS branch chairman Mrs Julia Hawksley and her husband, the Reverend W. Hawksley, and Norah O'Shea. The proceedings opened with several musical interludes and the meeting then got down to business. Lady Frances Balfour moved and the motion was carried that the time had come when in the interests of the country, women of the United Kingdom should be enfranchised on the same terms as men. Copies of the resolution would be sent to the prime minister and his cabinet. Again, it was all to no avail. Constitutional tactics having failed militancy was resumed with a vengeance in 1909 and met now with increased resistance from the authorities.

The ensuing litany of scuffles with the police, allegations of brutality, arrests, court cases, prison sentences, hunger strikes and forced feeding was followed closely by the *Hampshire Telegraph* which had little sympathy for the seven women in Winson Green on hunger strike who suffered the indignity of forced feeding in late 1909,

> They had armed themselves with hatchets, smashed windows, unroofed houses, flung slates at policemen and had committed other outrages. They deserved severer punishment than had been inflicted upon them, and there was no earthly reason for not enforcing the ordinary prison discipline when they attempted to obtain their discharge by refusing food under the erroneous assumption that the lenient measures used to the women in prison in London would be extended to them. There is an end to the entire administration of justice if malefactors are to be let loose from prison provided they refuse to take food.

The Portsmouth branch of the NUWSS continued to deplore militant tactics roundly for putting back the cause of women's suffrage but clearly there was support locally for such ploys. Christabel Pankhurst herself visited Portsmouth during the abortive by-election campaign of 1909. The meeting she addressed in the Town Hall was packed out with an over-flow of almost 2,000 whom she addressed afterwards from the Town Hall steps.

Efforts were made throughout 1910 and 1911 to secure a constitutional solution to the issue of votes for women. There was a lull in hostilities. The Liberals had been returned to power, however, at the General Election in January 1910 without an overall majority. Instinctive intransigence combined now with determination to hold on to power whatever the cost in terms of militant action. Convinced that any measure of women's suffrage would hand over thousands of votes to the Conservatives, Liberal manoeuvring ensured that initiative after initiative by suffragist Members of Parliament was defeated. Finally, in late November 1911, the latest Conciliation Bill was effectively torpedoed by Asquith's proposed Manhood Suffrage Bill to be so drafted that it could be amended, if the Commons wished, to include the enfranchisement of women.

Not everyone thought the Conciliation Bill was lost. At a meeting organised in Portsmouth by the local branch of the NUWSS to look at what was on offer under the proposed Government Bill, speakers advocated taking what was on offer and capitalising on this, 'the thin end of the wedge'. A few days later there was a report of another meeting at which Norah O'Shea announced that the branch would be holding meetings in all the municipal wards over the next three months in support of the Conciliation Bill which they did not believe was lost yet. Meetings took place throughout February and March. Once again Lady Selborne was a prominent speaker. It was up-hill work though. Thoroughly disillusioned now with the government's failure to take them seriously, WSPU members had resumed militant tactics with a vengeance. Mass breaking of windows in government buildings in Whitehall, and at Somerset House, the National Liberal Federation, the Guards' Club, a number of London hotels, the *Daily Mail* and *Daily News,* Swan and Edgar's and a number of other shops and businesses had taken place in November 1911 and in the New Year the attacks on private property escalated. Press reaction was swift locally and nationally. The *Hampshire Telegraph* declared that, the campaign of wanton destruction and wilful damage which has characterised the actions of the militant suffragists during the last few days, has amazed and disgusted even their own friends. What possible object can be served by such abominable conduct cannot be conceived, and surely in the calmer moments which are being prepared for the suffragette leaders they will reflect on the folly of such undertakings.

The Pethick-Lawrences and Mrs Pankhurst were arrested now on charges of conspiracy. The hearing into the conspiracy charges coincided with the second reading of the Conciliation Bill. It was lost by just fourteen votes. The Pethick-Lawrences and Mrs Pankhurst were committed for trial. Christabel meanwhile escaped to France. The trial in May and the defendants' subsequent imprisonment provoked a public outcry. The WSPU recovered some of the sympathy it had lost and in fact many of the women including the hunger-strikers were released before the expiry of their sentences. The Pethick-Lawrences urged caution now and advocated consolidating the sympathy engendered by the trial but Christabel from her refuge in France was determined to continue the militant campaign. The first serious arson attack took place on 13 July 1912 at Nuneham House in Oxfordshire, the home of government minister Lewis Harcourt, Secretary for the Colonies.

There was a lull in militancy in January 1913 during the debates on the Manhood Suffrage Bill. Portsmouth suffragists had spent the previous six months campaigning for women's suffrage amendments to the Bill. Local MPs were called upon and urged to support the amendments, and at a large meeting in the Town Hall Square in Portsmouth, organised by the NUWSS, a resolution was put and carried by the crowd urging the Portsmouth members, both Conservative, 'to vote for the deletion of the word 'male' from the Franchise Bill.' From his pulpit in the High Street Unitarian Chapel, the minister, Mr Thompson, urged his congregation to pray that the prime minister and the government might have wisdom when the matter came to be debated in Parliament. Once again, it was a waste of time. The Speaker ruled on 23 January that the insertion of the women's suffrage amendment clauses so altered the bill as to necessitate its withdrawal.

The WSPU was beside itself with rage and frustration. Slogans were daubed on buildings and burned into bowling greens, telegraph and telephone lines were cut, windows were smashed in London clubs, an orchid house was burned down in Kew Gardens and the restaurant in Regent's Park destroyed by fire. Most of the culprits escaped but Mrs Pankhurst was arrested for procuring and inciting women to commit offences contrary to the Malicious Injuries to Property Act 1861. She was sentenced in April to three years' penal servitude. Public and press reaction was universally hostile. As the campaign of destruction continued into the spring, the opposition to the women became more violent. Meetings were broken up by hostile crowds and individuals were attacked on the streets. It is against this background that Portsmouth women took part in the Great Non-Militant March to London in July 1913, 'the object of which was to show that the non-militants were as anxious to receive political recognition as the militants'. Some measure of the strength of the opposition to the militants is clear in the diary which survives of Harriet Blessley who took part in the march. It is obvious that for Harriet, the daughter of a Portsmouth businessman, the march assumed the proportions of a spiritual and moral crusade or pilgrimage. The women stayed with local sympathisers along the way.

The Portsmouth contingent left the Town Hall Square at 5.00 p.m. on 17 July 1913,

> Marched off round back of Town Hall to front, and up the road. Hot and smelly. Hemmed in with back streeters and boys running in between police. Band played march to suit masculine strides; had hard job to keep up .... A cheer or two and one tomatoe [sic] on my hat. Reach boundary. Police leave us. March some distance unescorted. Cosham police (three) take charge outside

*The walkers leave Portsmouth Town Hall Square, 17 July 1913. Author's Collection*

Cosham. Inhabitants excited and displeased. ('Go home and mend your stockings!' 'Where's Mrs Pankhurst?') 'You'll drop dead before you reach London!' Reach field adjoining Miss O'Shea's house. Blessed green grass and rest! Labour Party strong. Rev'd Thompson spoke to crowd outside hedge. Sang! Three cheers for Cause, Labour Party and Pilgrims.

At Petersfield there were, in the words of the *Hampshire Telegraph,* 'unparalleled scenes'. Poor Harriet was caught up in the thick of it,

Meeting in Market Square at 8.15 p.m. Chair taken by Vicar, who it appears is very unpopular. Crowd won't listen. Cannot convince them we are not militant. Miss O'Shea speaks, but shouting and hissing prevent her being heard … Labour man tries his hand … No avail.

*They pass the Charles Dickens Birthplace, 17 July 1913. Author's Collection*

*Walking through Petersfield, 18 July 1913. Author's Collection*

## SUFFRAGISTS' HUNTED.

## PORTSMOUTH PILGRIMS.

## MEETING BROKEN UP.

### DISORDERLY PETERSFIELD SCENES

The arrival in Petersfield yesterday of the contingent of Women Suffrage Pilgrims from Portsmouth aroused great public interest; and in the evening when an attempt was made to hold a meeting in the Market-square, unparalleled scenes were witnessed and the Suffragists met with a very hostile reception.

The Pilgrims reached the town about seven o'clock, and were met in the Causeway by a good many members of the Petersfield Women's Suffrage Society. The processionists, carrying banners and wearing colour of the National Union of Women's Suffrage Societies, numbered about fifty. They marched to the Square without interference, followed by a big crowd of people; and Miss N. O'Shea having addressed a few words of thanks for their reception, the Suffragists dispersed for what they were evidently in need of after their long tramp —rest and refreshment. An hour later the public meeting was fixed to begin. As enormous crowd had collected, and from the start it was evident that a considerable section meant to prevent the speakers getting a hearing.

The Rector (the Rev. Archdall M, Hill) managed with great difficulty to explain some of the reasons why he supported this movement. He was subjected to constant interruption, the crowd in front of him booing and shouting to such an extent that only those in his immediate vicinity could hear him. There were frequent cries of "Have a banana!" A reference to an appeal by the Rector in a recent number of the parish magazine, which created much amusement; and "The Boys," as they termed themselves, several times broke into the refrain of a well-known song with that title. Eventually, finding it useless to continue, Mr. Hill stopped speaking.

Dr. Leachman tried to make an appeal for fair play, but the crowd positively refused to hear him; and Miss O'Shea fared little better, though she continued to talk amid the din for some time. Mr. Montague Fordham then had a try, but all to no purpose.

The Suffragists at last gave up trying altogether, and endeavoured to get away. The excited mob, however, were by this time worked up to such a pitch that they were not in a mood to cease their disorder, and some ugly rushes were made towards the waggonette which the speakers had been occupying. This was nearly over-turned, but was eventually got out of the Square. The police, under Supt. Garrett, acted with discretion, and did their best to protect the women, who were being hustled and were in some danger. Most of these got away safely, but one or two were followed by dense throngs of boys and young men, and the police had no light task in keeping off their tormentors, and giving them a chance to reach the houses where they were staying.

The crowd in the Square must have numbered over a thousand, and for some time gangs were rushing from one point to another in the Square and the adjacent streets, hunting for Suffragettes. There was a bit of a demonstration in front of the Rectory, but before ten o'clock things had quieted down, and most of the people had dispersed. No such scene of excitement and disorder has probably been witnessed before in the town, and the assemblage of people was quite one of the biggest on record. At one period it seemed likely that personal injury might result from the swaying of the mob, but happily nobody was hurt. The Pilgrims are not likely soon to forget the treatment meted out to them in Petersfield, and the demonstration cannot be regarded as creditable to the town. The meeting held in the same place the previous evening by the anti-Suffragists was, by contrast, a striking success.

Miss O'Shea asks for literature. Not having enough 'Protests against Militancy', I go to wagonette in stable at end of High Street to get some more. Come back and find meeting dispersing, Cannot find my party or hostess. Run into a hooligan crowd, who try to snatch my collecting box and leaflets. Policeman comes to my rescue, and escorts me through crowd to the Hotel... Crowd follows and waits outside. My hostess joins me, and we wait inside, till crowd disperses, and sneak out with colours down. I feel a coward. Feel more firmly non-militant, seeing the fierce animosity caused by the militants.

The following day, 19 July 1913, the party reached Haslemere. At Liphook, where they had lunched en route, Lady Selborne had given them a rallying address, 'rather badly' in Harriet's view. She felt, she wrote, 'like a real pilgrim going to a Holy Shrine' in the Market Square in Haslemere. There was more trouble in Guildford,

Enormous crowd …. Booing and jeering. Go round selling 'Common Cause', and distribute leaflets. Many people annoyed who want to listen but hooligans prevent …. Feel so wild with stupid crowd. Police rush in and bundle off a party. After that a little quiet and a few words got in. Corner of crowd gets angry. Police surround wagonette, Crowd surges forward. Women faint…. Police advise speakers to stop, which

*Newscutting from the* Evening Mail *reporting on the violence the women met in Petersfield, 18 July 1913. Portsmouth History Centre*

they reluctantly do…. The old story – we are taken for militants. It is difficult to feel a holy pilgrim when one is called a brazen hussy.

Sheltering from the rain in the porch of an inn near Cobham, Harriet and her companion were amused to hear the landlord discussing them,

> Racing all over the country – what's their poor wretched men doin' of? We tell him what we tell people a hundred times a day – that we are not militant, and ask him to read a leaflet and see what we really *do* believe, but he turns purple with rage and flings our leaflet to the ground.

They noticed, however, that the nearer they got to London, 'the more intelligent and tolerant the crowd'. Someone even cried 'Stick to it, girls!' as they crossed Hammersmith Bridge. The march culminated in a huge rally in Hyde Park on 26 July. There were nineteen platforms and the Surrey, Sussex and Hampshire one was chaired by Norah O'Shea.

However, as Harriet and her fellow-walkers discovered, nothing – and certainly not the Great Non-Militant March – could convince the general public that suffrage campaigners

*The image above and the next three come from a small scrapbook of news cuttings, possibly from the* Portsmouth Times, *recording the women's progress. Here, wearing academic dress and suffrage sashes, the women are jeered by the crowd in either Portsmouth or Petersfield, 17 or 18 July 1913. Portsmouth History Centre*

*Marching cheerfully and resolutely, n.d.*

were not all militants. The arson campaign continued through the winter. At the end of December there was a serious fire in Portsmouth Dockyard. The Semaphore Tower collapsed, the Rigging House and Sail Loft were gutted and two men lost their lives. Strong rumours circulated locally that the fire was

*Washing up and tidying 'the camp', n.d.*

*Crossing Hammersmith Bridge, 25 July 1913.*

the work of militants. The *Hampshire Telegraph* reported that 'it is even said that some little time ago a letter was received from the women's militant organisation threatening such an outbreak'. Nothing was ever proved though and the authorities said the fire was due to the fusing of electric wires – and the notion that women could even have gained access to the site was very firmly discounted.

The damage done to property and the scale of the violence on the London streets in the New Year and early months of 1914 was unprecedented. There was a furious editorial in the *Hampshire Telegraph* on 13 March 1914 when the news broke of the slashing of Velazquez's *Rokeby Venus* in the National Gallery,

> The completely senseless damaging of a nation's art treasure can do nothing other than create in the minds of reasonable people contempt for the individuals concerned, and for the form of reasoning which has given rise to the utterly unconstitutional and criminal practices which have lately become all too frequent, without helping the cause of women's suffrage one iota.

*The Great Dockyard Fire as seen from The Common Hard, 20 December 1913. Author's Collection.*

Meetings of local suffragists were broken up now by irate crowds throughout the spring and early summer. There is little doubt that the outbreak of war on 4 August 1914 was a blessing for the WSPU and its leaders. They had manoeuvred themselves into an impossible situation. They had alienated not only politicians hitherto sympathetic to their cause but also many of their own members, and had played right into the hands of the die-hard anti-suffragists.

There was in fact no real militancy in Portsmouth or its immediate area. There were no outrages committed. Fred Blessley, Harriet's brother, broke a window in the Town Hall in June 1913 but that seems to have been the limit of militant activity in Portsmouth. In fact, if the local newspapers are any guide, most suffrage activists in Portsmouth were appalled by the excesses of the militants. The ways in which local women went about achieving their ends were not particularly remarkable by today's standards but then it was unusual for women to form exclusive organisations and tackle an issue so single-mindedly. If you look at the Annual Reports of the Victoria Nursing Association or the Rescue Society there is always a cadre of men who constitute the core officers and organising committee. Women, and women only, called public meetings on the issue of women's suffrage, planned the campaigns, lobbied local MPs, spoke on street corners, raised money for their cause, sold suffrage literature and marched to make their point.

The local branch of the NUWSS even had its own headquarters by November 1913 when two rooms were opened officially at 2, Kent Road, Southsea. Money was raised at jumble sales, sales of work, collections at public meetings and in the streets. Little is known of any individual women who played significant roles in the campaign other than the O'Shea sisters and Lady Selborne. None of these ladies should be underestimated though particularly Norah O'Shea. She features time and again in the pages of the local newspapers: calling meetings, sending letters for printing to the Editor, addressing groups and, with her sister, organising fundraising events (the garden parties at East Cosham Cottage were legendary and still talked about fifty years later). She headed deputations and lead her followers – and her own maids – on the Great Non-Militant March in summer 1913. Whether Portsmouth was an important provincial centre, as Lancelot Surry claimed, is difficult to prove for lack of evidence. All that can be said with impunity is that the local branch of the NUWSS was far more active in the suffrage campaign than recent historians have suspected. Certainly, described in 1913 as 'the worst sweated town in the three kingdoms', Portsmouth should have been very fertile territory for the suffrage societies and indeed when war broke out in August 1914 plans were well in hand to hold a huge protest meeting against sweating. The strong tradition of female independence in a community used to their men spending long periods of time away from home should also have been an influential factor but the extraordinary thing is that there is no evidence that these factors had any profound effect at all on the fight for the vote here. The Portsmouth campaign seems to have been middle-class through and through.

## CHAPTER SIX

# War

***

Brickwoods came to the rescue of some of the corset girls put out of work in the early weeks of the war, engaging thirty-two to replace young men who had joined up. In the ensuing weeks and months, as more young men enlisted, increasing numbers of women took their places. They worked across the town, for the Relief Committee itself in the Town Hall; for the Red Cross, as Voluntary Aid Detachments (VADs), many in local hospitals, and in local industrial undertakings. Nowhere would this be more startling and totemic than in Portsmouth Dockyard. By 1917 it would be impossible to deny women's claims for the vote.

Rumours of spies – German spies – abounded, particularly rumours of glamourous female ones, as a roundup of foreign nationals took place a few days after the outbreak of war. Most foreign nationals had in fact been identified already and the Chief Constable was empowered to detain and search the premises of anyone suspicious. If the individual was suspect, he or she was detained and handed over to the Special Branch. Several alleged spies were arrested including a girl in Pelham Road, Southsea. She may have been the young woman alluded to by Fred T. Jane, the naval analyst and sometime intelligence officer of *Fighting Ships* fame, who lived in Southsea. He expressed regret that he and an army officer 'had sent an awfully pretty girl to limbo. Having done it, we asked each other – Don't you feel an awful swine?'

More fortunate was local schoolgirl Gwendoline Kyffin, the 17-year-old daughter of Southsea GP and local Territorial, Dr John Kyffin who would in due course become Commanding

Officer of the 5th Southern General Hospital. Gwendoline was enjoying a holiday on the Rhine with two friends when war broke out. The girls got separated somehow; the newspaper accounts of what happened are not clear on a number of points. After a brief period of house arrest near Bonn, Gwendoline decided to make her own way home by whatever means offered. She walked some twelve miles initially before being able to get a train. There was a brush with five drunken German troops at some stage when she had a bayonet pressed into her side, but somehow she managed to escape their attentions and after four days of travelling got home safely. She was fêted as a local heroine.

Portsmouth suffragists and suffragettes threw themselves into the war effort from the beginning of hostilities. As their brothers enlisted, and remarkably Portsmouth raised three battalions of 1,000 men apiece in the first months of the war, the younger women raised significant sums of money on flag days and at other fundraising events. They also enrolled as VADs. The organisation was founded in 1909 with the help of the Red Cross and the Order of St John, and became a part of the Technical Reserve of the Territorial Army (TA) in 1910. Detachments were formed across the country and sufficient training took place to ensure that in the event of war, everyone knew what to do. When war did break out, Portsmouth VADs were ready. As the first wounded arrived in hospital trains, they met and disembarked the men, and drove them in ambulances to their designated hospital. It was important work that they did, among other things, throughout the war. One girl, Beryl Orde-Powlett, drove an astonishing 38,000 miles between 1916 and the end of the war in a Sunbeam car fitted with an ambulance body. This particular vehicle, according to Gates in *Portsmouth and the Great War*, carried some 43,000 patients, usually with Beryl Orde-Powlett at the wheel, during its time in service. It was attached to the 5th Southern General Hospital in Fawcett Road, the requisitioned former Boys' and Girls' Secondary Schools, and met all the Red Cross trains arriving at Fratton, Portsmouth Town and Cosham stations, and took patients to that hospital. Other VADs worked as nursing orderlies, cooks, kitchen maids, clerks, housemaids, ward maids and laundresses, many under the auspices of the Red Cross, in local hospitals but a number went abroad and worked in Field Hospitals on the French coast, as 'Tubby' Clayton discovered.

Philip 'Tubby' Clayton, who founded the club for troops, Talbot House ('Toc H') at Poperinghe in the Ypres salient in 1915, had been a curate under Garbett at St Mary's Portsea before the war. Like most of Garbett's curates he enlisted in the Chaplain-General's Department soon after war was declared. He was sent in due course to the 16th General Hospital British Expeditionary Force (BEF) which was at Le Tréport near Dieppe between 1915 and 1917 when it was taken over by the Americans. The British base hospitals were part of the casualty evacuation chain, further back from the front line than the casualty clearing stations, usually accessible by railway, and near a channel port. In his letters home to Garbett which were published in the parish magazine, Clayton writes of a huge

107   GUERRE DE 1914. — A Portsmouth. — Arrivée de blessés
      Al Portsmouth. — Arrival of English wounded

Reproduction interdite
LL.

*Arrival of Wounded at Portsmouth, n.d. Author's Collection.*

hospital under canvas, high on the cliff tops, close to the sea. He was allotted a marquee to set up a church, and with help from a convalescent patient, they made an altar of ward lockers, and Communion rails. He established a system of services, and observed with pleasure his congregations growing week on week particularly at his mission services on the cliff top at 7.00 p.m. on Sunday evenings. He also discovered that there were at least two Southsea girls among the VADs.

One of the most impressive pieces of war work tackled in Portsmouth in the first months of the war was organised initially by a small group of Royal Navy officers' wives. They knew that many ships' companies had failed to allot their pay to their wives before war broke out. Ships were now leaving with no notice at all, often in the middle of the night, and the Relief Committee in the Town Hall, managed by Miss Kelly and her team of volunteer ladies, was overwhelmed with requests from sailors' wives and families for financial assistance. Mrs Bradford, wife of Vice-Admiral Edward Bradford, volunteered with Miss Blewitt, daughter of the garrison commander, to do what they could to help. Mrs Bradford suggested that the whole town should be divided up into its constituent parishes, and that a house-to-house visitation should be undertaken and a register compiled of all the naval wives and families. A useful contemporary typescript account survives detailing the initiative.

Mrs Bradford went herself to the parish of St James's Milton in the south-east corner of Portsea Island. Milton had been an isolated farming settlement until new Marine Barracks were built there 1862–7. By the time of the First World War, it was a community of some 23,000 inhabitants – mainly the families of naval men, Marines and dockyard workers. Other than the Marine officers and their families, there were very few business and professional people of independent means. With the help of the Vicar of St James's Church, Milton, Mrs Bradford was able to recruit a number of parishioners with time to spare from what the vicar called their 'daily work and household duties' who agreed to carry out the initial house-to-house visitations, each of them taking a given number of adjoining streets. Mrs Bradford

Rentals of Houses 6/- to 20/- weekly.   Rentals from 6/- to 10/- largely predominating.

No leisured residents.

Four Clergy of Church of England, very few Ministers of other denominations.

### Development of Work

The Vicar of Milton called a meeting of those of his parishioneers who might have some time to spare from daily work and household duties.

Mrs Bradford read an extract from a letter from her husband, Vice Admiral E. Bradford, commanding a Battle Squadron at sea. "So glad you are sharing in the great and useful work that the women have undertaken that is a splendid stimulant to us, it is a relief to all here to think that those who can are assisting those in need".

Seventy of those present undertook to carry out a house to house visitation, each taking a given number of adjoining streets.   Mrs Bradford drew up and had printed a simple registration card, to give name and address of naval man's nearest relation, his rating name of his ship and his official number.  (This card was subsequently copied and used in other places and also for soldiers families)

In the course of ten days all houses had been visited, registration cards filled in and re urned to Mrs Bardford and Miss Blewitt who with the help of five friends, relations of naval officers, made an alphabetical register of the names received, approximately nine hundred, with particulars.   They made a further list of Streets, seventy five streets in the Parish with names and addresses in alphabetical order for the use of visitors; also register of the names of H.M.Ships, with

*Extract from the 'Report on Work in Milton', c.1920. Portsmouth History Centre.*

the names and addresses of relations of men serving in each
ship. (When the tide of casualties came this was found
invaluable for immediate knowledge of those in trouble)  These
Registers have since had to be increased by a sad record of
widows, orphans and other dependents of men lost on active
service.

Mrs Bradford having been reinforced by five more friends,
every naval man's nearest relation living in Milton was visited
in a very short time.   Many were the troubles discovered.
The main dificulty being the voluntary system of pay to the
wives, which constituted the sole means of subsistence, men had
been in the habit of sending pay home by postal orders, ships
had gone off at a moments notice, no one knew where, no letters
were being received, no money forthcoming.   The wives of naval
reservists were in even worse case, unused to separation from
their husbands, the dificulties were often more bewildering.

Visitors were able to put all cases in need in touch with
relief.   Prompt financial help was given through the H.S.F.A
or other agencies.   Milton being an outlying district
applicants for assistance were often unable to go to the S&S.F.A
Offices at Portsmouth Town Hall themselves, and M$^R$s Bradford
and her helpers were appointed almoners for S & S. F. A and
N. Royal Patriotic Fund, reporting cases to the local committees
and taking relief back to Milton. But very many were the cases
where help from relief funds was not needed, though advice,
friendship and sympathy were urgently called for.   The condition
were abnormal, the bewilderment and anxiety great.  One of the
services most frequently rendered and most appreciated was to
put men's wives into touch with the wives of officers serving in
the same ship, a bond of fellowship was formed and confidence giv

*Main Gates, Portsmouth Dockyard, c.1916. Author's Collection.*

*Portsmouth Dockyard in 1916. Author's Collection.*

designed and had printed a simple registration card with space for the naval man's nearest relation, rating, the name of his ship and his official number. It took the team of women ten days to visit all the houses in the parish. The completed cards were returned to Mrs Bradford and her small group of officers' wives and friends who between them made an alphabetical register of the names received with their particulars. There were over 900 names. They also made a list of streets, seventy-five in all, with the names and addresses of the residents, in alphabetical order, for the use of visitors, and a register of ships with the names and addresses of the relations of the men serving in each one. These proved to be invaluable tools for identifying quickly those families which would need help when lists of casualties came through.

With their lists now completed, Mrs Bradford's team set to and visited each registered family. As anticipated, the main difficulty was to do with pay,

> the voluntary system of pay to the wives, which constituted the sole means of subsistence , men had been in the habit of sending pay home by postal orders, ships had gone off at a moment's notice, no one knew where, no letters were being received, no money forthcoming. The wives of naval reservists were in even worse case, unused to separation from their husbands, the difficulties were often more bewildering.

All cases in need were put in touch with the relevant caring agency. Often the officers' wives acted as lady almoners for the latter bodies, doing the necessary reporting and bringing back of information and material help. Milton was an outlying area and if wives had small children it was not easy to get to the Town Hall and the relief offices. Money was in fact identified before long to pay for a 'resident worker' in the parish. Miss Marian Edwards came to Milton in September 1914 and was still there three years later, urging the appointment of a second worker. It was impossible to over-estimate what she had meant to the naval population of Milton in the time she was with them said the typescript report,

> She is accessible at all times to those in trouble and no exertion on her part that could serve to alleviate distress has ever been spared. Typical of the feelings towards her was the remark made by a Milton inhabitant at the close of a debate on 'What good can come out of the War?' 'It has already brought one good in Miss Edwards'.

What Mrs Bradford and her different teams of women did was put in place a system which would ensure that no sailor's wife would find herself without a confidante or friend should she receive the news they all dreaded of their husband – or son's – death. It was a system which was soon copied for soldiers' families as well. It was a timely intervention as on 1 September 1914 the first batch of wounded from the British Expeditionary Force (BEF) arrived at Fratton Station; 120 sick and wounded were taken off the train by VADs in nine private cars and the Borough Police motor ambulances, and taken to the hospital in Fawcett Road. It was not long either before news of the Battle of Coronel and the loss of most of the South Atlantic Squadron under Rear Admiral Sir Christopher Cradock reached England. The battle had been fought almost on the other side of the world, off the coast of central Chile on 1 November 1914. The tragedy appalled the country. There were many local men and boys on board Cradock's flag ship HMS *Good Hope* which was lost with all hands. It was the first British naval defeat since 1812. Revenge was exacted swiftly with the assembly in Portsmouth, and rapid despatch to the South Atlantic, of a hastily-scrambled naval force under the pugnacious Vice Admiral Doveton Sturdee. Local losses at Coronel were harbingers, however, of much worse to come.

With the fall of Antwerp on 10 October 1914 came the news that 2,000 British troops were now prisoners of war having crossed the frontier into Holland. Among the POWs were members of the Naval Brigade, many Portsmouth men.

They finished up in Doeberitz, a large prison camp eight miles outside Berlin. Three thousand men were interned here, most were English and were captured at Antwerp. Food was in desperately short supply and the men were heavily dependent on food parcels sent from home. One or two local women whose husbands and sons were prisoners at Doeberitz began in a small way sending parcels of food in late 1914 and early 1915. They worked unofficially from their own homes and underwrote the enterprise themselves but, as the numbers of local men captured and incarcerated increased, by 1916 the cost of the operation had spiralled beyond the ladies' means and it was put onto an official footing. The Portsmouth Prisoners of War Fund was established with the Mayor of Portsmouth, Councillor Corke, as chairman. A committee was formed and funds raised through flag days, collections in schools, churches and work places, at whist drives, and at concerts and matinée performances in local theatres. Weekly social gatherings were organised by the committee for the wives and mothers of POWs at St Mary's Mission Hall in Fratton Road. Over tea and an entertainment news could be exchanged. At their Christmas party in 1916 – there were 400 people present – a photograph was taken and a copy sent in their Christmas parcel to each man in captivity. It cost 6s. to send a parcel and its contents in 1916. This amounted to monthly expenditure in the region of £200 (£16,000 today). By the end of the war, this sum had risen to £600 a month. This was a considerable sum of money (almost £50,000 today). It was raised consistently each month in addition to the many other fundraising initiatives by a tireless group of volunteers, most of whom were women.

Many of them freely admitted that volunteering was a welcome distraction from worrying about husbands and sons imperilled far from home but they were also driven by patriotic fervour. Mrs Charles of Southsea was an indefatigable pre-war fundraiser for any number of charitable endeavours. She now redirected her energies to the war effort, raising significant sums initially for the National Relief Fund in one of the first flag days to be organised in the town. She and her fellow-volunteers made and sold tiny, hand-painted Union Jack flags in the streets. They also collected clothing for Belgian refugees given sanctuary in the Portsmouth area, and when the wounded began arriving at local railway stations, she not only met trains, day and night, distributing cigarettes and sweets to each man but collected tobacco products and sweets, and walking sticks, soap and tooth brushes which were taken to local hospitals.

The American wife of the commanding officer on the Gunwharf, Mrs Slade-Baker, also contributed significantly to the local war effort. She and her band of helpers collected enough money and materials in the first six months of the war to contribute handsomely not only to ten Red Cross hospitals in Portsmouth and its immediate neighbourhood, but also to a number in France and Belgium. They sent bedsteads, blankets, sheets, pillow-cases, water-bottles, slippers, dressing-gowns, pyjamas, bed-jackets, scarves, woollen helmets, mittens, boots and overcoats, and huge quantities of medical supplies. Mrs Slade-Baker and her team of ladies also filled thousands of sandbags, as did Mrs Arnold Foster's team, in their war work depot in Highbury Street. They also made and collected items of clothing and other goods for soldiers and sailors, hospitals and hospital ships. They made shirts and socks, and like Mrs Slade-Baker's ladies, made slippers, trench-slippers, operation socks and pneumonia jackets. They also made treasure bags for wounded men to put their small belongings in when they set off on the often long journey home. Paradoxically, as discussed already, it was this considerable volunteer effort which put the girls in the different dress trades in Portsmouth out of work in the early months of the war, when they could have been usefully employed manufacturing much of this material. Norah O'Shea and the local branch of the NUWSS were more than aware of this dichotomy.

There was a Surgical and Medical Depot at Lennox Mansions in Southsea run by Miss Bevington. She and her team made bandages in all shapes and sizes, swabs and limb pillows. They used sphagnum moss in the preparation of their dressings. With its absorptive and very acidic properties, it inhibited the growth of bacteria. Considerable quantities of such medical supplies were shipped to France through the energy and determination of Mrs Marion Wyllie, the wife of Royal Academician W.L. Wyllie. She and her husband lived at Tower House on Portsmouth Point near the Round Tower. They began war work immediately war was declared. In her autobiography, *We Were One*, Marion Wyllie wrote that she was 'backwards and forwards through France with what, in the end, totalled 89 tons of hospital supplies and comforts for the wounded and suffering'.

She had been prompted to act when she received a letter in October 1914 from a friend telling her of the awful conditions in two hospitals, one in Dieppe and another well behind the lines in Limoges. The Dieppe hospital had 500 wounded with only two doctors and one nurse to care for them. The men were dying from tetanus, septic wounds and gangrene. Within a week, with the help of friends, working in her husband's studio, Mrs Wyllie had packed a number of enormous bales of medical supplies and was on her way to France with Miss Bevington on the Red Cross Yacht *Medusa* which the ladies secured through the good offices of the Portsmouth Commander-in-Chief's Flag Captain. For two years the ladies crossed to France every two months with tons of stores for different hospitals on the French lines. Bales of hospital supplies were also sent out to the Red Cross hospital in the port of Mudros on the Greek island of Lemnos in the Aegean. Allied casualties were brought here before the full evacuation of the Gallipoli peninsula took place in 1915. Mrs Arnold Forster was treasurer for the hospital and with the £1,000 her team of ladies raised annually in Southsea for the hospital, Mrs Wyllie sent out clothing, comforts, surgical dressings, food, blankets, beds and cigarettes.

As the war progressed and the numbers of casualties grew increasing amounts of accommodation had to be identified locally and turned over to their care. The secondary schools in Fawcett Road were followed by Sir John Brickwood's mansion in Kent Road, 'Brankesmere', and Mr Frank Bevis's large house, 'Oatlands' on Kingston Crescent. Both gentlemen cheerfully surrendered their property for the good of the cause. In due course the Royal Hospital had to hand over three wards to the military, and the Board of Guardians handed over the entire Infirmary at Milton. The Infectious Diseases Hospital at Milton was also surrendered and the Eye and Ear Hospital in Pembroke Road. With other establishments in the Portsmouth hinterland they made up together the 5th Southern General Hospital. There were 300 beds at the beginning of the war. By the end there were 2,200 and the different sites treated some 38,000 casualties. Gwendoline Kyffin's father, now Territorial Colonel John Kyffin was the Commanding Officer until he went to Salonica in 1916. Territorial Nursing Service Sisters were employed initially to do nursing work and were supplemented in due course by Red Cross VADs. Local VADs also worked as cooks and cleaners. Mounting casualties also meant that the demand for fighting men grew and more women were recruited to replace them, not in back offices but in munition factories and in the dockyard itself, as discussed in an earlier chapter.

Portsmouth's *annus horribilis* was the year 1916. Six Portsmouth naval ships: the battle-cruisers *Queen Mary* and *Invincible,* the cruiser *Black Prince,* and the destroyers *Ardent, Fortune* and *Sparrowhawk* were lost at the Battle of Jutland on 31 May 1916. Four thousand, mainly local, men were lost and 1,500 homes were left fatherless. As if this was not bad enough less than a week later HMS *Hampshire,* another Portsmouth ship, hit a mine and sank off the mainland of Orkney in mountainous seas with Lord Kitchener on board. She had a complement of 655 officers and men, and only a handful survived. On land more disaster befell the town when news reached their families that of the three volunteer battalions – over 3,000 young men altogether – recruited in the early weeks of the war who marched off so proudly and confidently to complete their training with the Hampshires, not one battalion returned. The men who survived the carnage of the fighting on the Somme, which began on 1 July 1916, were assimilated in due course into the depleted ranks of other regiments. There could not have been a family in the town which was not directly or indirectly affected by this slaughter of its men.

Never, said Gates, had more distressing scenes been witnessed in the town than on the night news of Jutland came through. He was in the offices of the *Evening News*. They were about to go home. There was a warning tick on their telegraph machine which indicated that a message was coming through. The words 'GREAT BATTLE IN THE NORTH SEA' were flashed through and the staff in the office saw in horror the names of the ships lost, most of which were Portsmouth ships. The news spread through the town like wildfire. Teams in the Town Hall worked through the night to give what help they could to distressed women and their families. The following day Miss Kelly and her Town Hall team set out to visit each widow in her own home where they could assure her that the Admiralty would continue to pay separation allowance as before for six months and by that time, pensions would be ready. An account also survives of the work of Mrs Bradford's team visiting now in Milton. 'The losses in the Jutland Bank Battle fell terribly hard on Portsmouth and

*HMS* Hampshire, *n.d. Author's Collection.*

the shock was appalling', noted the writer. They visited everyone mourning the death of a husband or son on the morning the news was confirmed 'and all that could be done was done to bring any possible comfort and relief'. There were fifty-one Jutland losses in Milton parish alone. Specific issues were reported to the Town Hall and relief organised such as nourishing food for a number of women ill from shock. Another woman was helped with the costs of her confinement with a posthumous child, and with food both before and after the baby's birth. One poor woman was contending not only with the news of her husband's death but six children ill with infectious diseases. She was given domestic help for the duration of their illness.

'All these and very many other cases of particular trouble need to be constantly befriended', the writer advised. A Memorial Service for those who lost their lives in the North Sea and on HMS *Hampshire* was held in St Mary's Portsea on Friday evening 9 June 1916. This church 'has never contained a

*St Mary's Church, Portsea, n.d. Author's Collection.*

sadder congregation than that which assembled there on Friday evening', said the report in the *Portsmouth Times*. The building was filled to capacity, and there was not a row where someone was not quietly weeping for their loss. A number of the Milton visitors became increasingly concerned in early 1917 about what they called 'the cumulative shock' of the dreadful losses in their area: the daily news of not only their own family bereavements but also the news of neighbours' losses. Some visitors even felt that the health of children was being prejudiced by their mothers' depression. Doctors recommended where possible 'change of occupation, cheerful surroundings, and congenial companionship', but this was not exactly practical advice for most people. However, with the help and advice of Miss Kelly's ladies in the Town Hall, an initiative was launched in 1917 to establish a Home Industry for Naval War Widows in Portsmouth which would make children's and ladies' clothing by hand as well as a range of embroidered items. A suitable property at 101, Winter Road was purchased, furnished and equipped to provide three workrooms, a showroom, a small office and kitchen. The enterprise was launched on 8 January 1918. Eight widows and one orphan daughter started work at once. As word spread, growing numbers of women who had been widowed recently and their dependants applied for training and employment. The Home Industry was soon working to capacity with twenty-six full-time workers. Eight part-timers worked in their own homes.

Orders were taken for knitted coats, jumpers, sweaters and frocks; wraps in silk or wool; children's frocks, overalls and tunics; copies of old French and English embroideries, and chair seats. Boxes of goods were sent out on approval or for exhibition. The wives of successive Commanders-in-Chief took great personal interest in the project and helped to organise exhibitions of the clothes in London and elsewhere. Royal patronage was secured in due course and a London show room found in Clarges Street, Mayfair, off Piccadilly. The organisation was still busily employed in the early 1930s. By this time over 100 women and their dependants had been trained in the Winter Road workrooms. The original aim of the project had been to take grieving Milton women's minds off their plight, enable them to supplement their pensions and, in some cases, provide them with the means to earn a living. Miss Kelly noted with some pride in her first official report on the venture, that they had been successful on all three counts. Few of the first women involved were qualified needlewomen and they made astonishing progress. She could report with pleasure that she found,

> some of the widows who have been known to me as suffering severely from shock, and to some extent from inertia, working with very evident keenness and enjoyment. One widow in particular who has been considered by us practically unemployable on account of hemiphlegia [paralysis] on the right side promises to be the best worker of all.

Fundraising, food production and national service by non-combatants became the key features of life in the town now and for the remainder of the war. I have written elsewhere about the formidable volunteer effort mounted in Portsmouth by non-combatants, large numbers of whom were women and their children, and whether the epithet, 'Peoples' War', more usually applied to the Second World War, might equally be applied to the First World War. Local people fought a good fight on their own doorsteps and made a significant contribution to the war effort. A War Savings Committee was established, and in proportion to its size and population, no town contributed more generously to war loans. Between 1917 and the end of the war, four campaigns raised just over £4 million, an average of £20 per head of the local population. The town also rose to the challenge of food shortages, chiefly of grain, during 1917. The grain shortage was due mainly to the disruption of supplies caused by enemy submarines but bad harvests played a part. A Royal proclamation on 2 May urged the strictest economy and the avoidance of waste 'in the use of every species of grain', and Garbett urged his parishioners in the March edition of the *Portsea Parish Magazine* to accept 'this sacrifice' without complaint. The Borough Council set up an Economy Committee to preach economy in foodstuffs, the avoidance of waste and the collection of textile and metal scraps. A Food Control Committee was charged to prevent profiteering and to ensure that orders issued by the Ministry of Food were carried out, maximum prices for milk, meat and coal being fixed. Lectures and demonstrations were organised across the town on how to bake using 'wartime' flour, and prepare cheap and nutritious meals. The doctrine of food economy was in fact preached so successfully that Portsmouth's home bakers reduced weekly bread consumption locally to a record-breaking 3lb 1oz per head. As part of a four-week waste campaign in local schools, mothers sent their children in with an astonishing three tons of waste paper, 24,000 bottles, nearly 8 tons of metal scrap and 15cwt of rags. Food waste was collected from hotels and restaurants for pigswill and a small committee of ladies was formed to collect waste wool, cotton and paper which could be taken to depots in different parts of the borough.

The public were also urged to grow more food. Spare parcels of land were identified across the borough for cultivation and there was keen competition for allotments. Whole families devoted their energies to growing staple crops of potatoes and other root vegetables. Efforts also began to persuade young women to enrol in the Women's Land Army. Established in 1915, there was an even greater need for recruits to tackle a desperate situation. At a Women's National Service meeting in the Town Hall on 27 April speakers reminded listeners that out of every five loaves baked in this country, four were produced using imported wheat. We had beaten the Germans on the battlefield but they had the power to starve us into submission. Volunteers would get a free outfit and train fare, maintenance and 18$s$ a week (roughly £80 today). Further details could be obtained in local Post Offices. Portsmouth girls signed up with alacrity; in fact over half the girls recruited in Hampshire came from Portsmouth. Hampshire also recruited more young women into the Women's Land Army than any other 'provincial county', according to Gates.

Similar efforts went now into persuading young women in Portsmouth to join the Women's Army Auxiliary Corps (WAACS) and the Women's Royal Naval Service (Wrens). They were employed initially doing domestic work: cooking meals and waiting at table, and working in laundries in barracks and ward rooms across the town but it was not long before, of necessity, they were recruited to do a whole range of clerical and technical jobs such as driving ambulances, motor cars and light vans if they were WAACS, or working as engineers, electricians, photographers, draughtswomen, tracers and signallers if they were Wrens. The WAACS had a smart khaki-coloured coat-frock, greatcoat and cap. The Wrens had blue coat-frocks with sailor collars. On their caps in gilt letters were the initials WRNS. The Women's Royal Air Force (WRAF) was a section of the Wrens initially and became a separate force only a few months before the end of the war. They had a limited presence on Portsea Island as there was only one air-station, at Tipnor.

The work of Miss Kelly and her team of helpers at the Town Hall had increased significantly by 1917. Charged now to administer the Naval and Military War Pensions Act, their name had changed from the Relief Committee to the War Pensions Committee. A report on their work appeared in local newspapers in early January 1917. They had 15,000 families on their books. They were notified of all soldiers and sailors discharged, and of all grants made to these men. They also received information on all Portsmouth casualties, and details of pensions and gratuities payable to widows and dependents. With this information, a team of visitors kept in touch with the discharged men, and with the widows, orphans and dependents of those who had lost their lives.

The Town Hall team admitted women and children to special homes and institutions, boarded children out, and made emergency arrangements for the care of children to give their mothers respite care, or to obtain special hospital or other treatment. They were often entirely responsible for the care of motherless children and orphans. They also managed the arrangements for the further care of severely wounded and disabled men, a number of whom might need to go into hospital once more. The War Pensions Committee would make the necessary financial arrangements. They also helped men to retrain for civilian life and worked with the local Labour Exchange to find job opportunities for them.

The Annual Reports of the MOH, Dr Mearns Fraser, shed useful light on the health and wellbeing of the borough during the war, and indirectly on women's health generally. Due to his campaigning the Maternity and Child Welfare Centre was opened in 1915 and the Venereal Diseases Centre in 1916. He also challenged robustly ill-informed assumptions about the town,

> Some little time back some misguided persons were making wild statements as to the number of illegitimate births that would take place in this town, and calling for special provisions to be made for dealing with the babies. How ill-founded the anticipations were is shown by the fact that not only has there been no increase in the number of illegitimate births in the Borough but the number registered has actually been the lowest recorded for the past few years.

He does not suggest why this should be so but it is tempting to wonder if it was part and parcel of a general improvement in their lot for many women by this time: educational opportunities had improved immeasurably for ambitious girls, there was work, and despite the self-imposed restrictions on food, and then rationing, introduced in 1918, there was an equitable distribution of available supplies. On the whole he considered that the health of the borough was pretty good throughout the war with the death rates falling for the usual killers: tuberculosis, enteric fever, scarlet fever and diphtheria. He was concerned though about the pressure on available housing stock. Many dockyard workers brought their families with them to Portsmouth just as many soldiers and sailors had always done. This placed unprecedented pressure on available housing stock and, according to Dr Fraser, there had never been so much overcrowding. Housing had been a particular concern of his before the war and he regretted that it had been necessary to put on hold when war broke out the reconstruction scheme for Voller Street in Portsea. He would return to the subject again after the war, reminding the council that if they did not deal with slum clearance resolutely they would prejudice the future health of the borough and the sound reputation they currently enjoyed.

On 28 March 1917, Asquith, once the intransigent opponent of women's suffrage rose to his feet in the House of Commons and said,

> I think that some time ago I ventured to use the expression, 'Let the women work out their own salvation'. Well, Sir, they have carried it out during this War. How could we have carried on the War without them? Short of actually bearing arms in the field, there is hardly a service which has contributed or is contributing to the maintenance of our cause in which women have not been at least as active and efficient as men, and wherever we turn we see them doing work … which three years ago would have been regarded as falling exclusively within the province of men … I … believe that some measure of women's suffrage should be conferred.

Almost twelve months later the Representation of the People Act received the Royal Assent on 6 February 1918. Women aged 30 and over who were householders, the wives of householders, occupiers of property of £5 or more annual value or university graduates were enfranchised. In Portsmouth 45,000 women became entitled to vote.

However, the war was not yet over. The allies had begun intervening in the Russian Civil War in early 1918 in support of the White Russians who were loyal to the Tsar. They hoped to revive an Eastern Front in the fight with Germany, and eventually overthrow the Bolsheviks. The plight of the refugees dislocated by the Russian fighting was pitiful. One local woman, Miss Theodora Williams from St Wilfrid's Mission, one of the Portsea Mission Churches, was sent to the Angliskaya Mission, Buzuluk in Samara Government, on the edge of the Asiatic steppes in Eastern Russia. She was more than likely one of the team of almost a dozen lay women from the deaconesses' home, St Andrew's, who were permanent members of staff at St Mary's Portsea and its mission churches. Like Garbett's curates, Theodora wrote home and her letters were also published in the parish magazines.

The refugees were penniless and starving women and children. Their menfolk had usually been taken away to fight. After dreadful suffering the families were relocated to other 'governments', as the Russians usually called their provinces, often far from their original homes. They were quartered on local populations who were scarcely better off themselves. It is a seldom-reported subject. Theodora wrote that she was in charge of a workroom at the mission where the women pulled, sorted and cleaned wool, and then wove it into cloth or spun it for stockings; they also knitted and sewed. As Miss Kelly discovered in Milton, so did Theodora – that the women cheered up considerably with something useful to do, companionship and some money in return for their work.

Theodora also went into some detail in her letters about the countryside in which she was living which she was confident would delight Portsea children. She described watching a camel train from her windows, each animal pulling a rough little cart. Camels, she explained, were greatly used and very hardy. In winter, covered often in heavy frost, they drew sledges through deep snow. The landscape was vast, the level steppes stretching away to the far horizon, like a great, flat, green sea dotted here and there with little mud villages of 'incredible' poverty but always with a beautiful, white church topped with a silver or golden dome. Further, she said, in every house was an icon with a lamp in front of it 'and no Russian thought of entering a house without first doing reverence to it; and every small child crossed itself and bowed to the icon before and after eating, even before taking medicine!' She worked in the local hospital as well. Nearly all the Russian doctors had gone to the front, leaving huge districts without any medical provision. Their unit was made up of three doctors, eight nurses and two orderlies and they had care of an area the size of Belgium with hundreds of small villages.

There were memorable scenes in Portsmouth on the morning of the 11 November 1918 when news of the armistice came through. The Commander-in-Chief, Sir Stanley Colville, heard the news first, and at 7.00 a.m. notified the Mayor, Councillor John Timpson. A great shout went up from the parade ground at the Royal Naval Barracks at 9.00 a.m. The 'General Assembly' had been sounded at 8.40 a.m. and all officers and men, including the Wrens, fell in in double-quick time. The news was announced by Rear-Admiral Pelly that an armistice had been signed: 'Officers and men, and others, I think this is not only an occasion for three cheers but for a yell. Now yell!'

*Peace Celebrations in Portsmouth, November 1918. Author's Collection.*

And yell they did, until they were hoarse, according to Gates. The Union Jack was broken as the National Anthem was sung, and a victory psalm and prayer were afterwards recited. Further cheers were given, and finally the Band played 'Land of Hope and Glory.' Hopefully the Wrens did not object to being referred to as 'others'.

## CHAPTER SEVEN

# After the war –
# and unfinished business…

### ✳✳✳

Portsmouth was the first town in the country in which the new electorate voted – and a woman was returned. Miss Kate Edmonds, sponsored by the Portsmouth Women Citizens' Association, was elected for St Simon's Ward in a municipal by-election on 17 November 1918 with a majority of more than 600 votes. 'And rightly so', said Gates, 'as her whole life was devoted to social service and welfare.' Thanking the returning Officer, she said that she took her return,

> not as a personal affair, but as a tribute to her sex, for what they (the women) had done in the war. (Hear, hear.) They had done her the honour of sending her to the Council; and the voters had shown how they felt their responsibility, for there were only a few spoilt votes. 'I will try and do my best to be faithful to the great obligation you have put upon me, and I feel very proud of the honour you have done me,' she concluded amid applause.

Some women had been able to vote in borough elections since 1869 but could not, of course, stand as candidates. The first woman parliamentary candidate was not so successful though. Miss Alison Garland stood as the Labour candidate

# Portsmouth Trades Council & Labour Party.

## Guardians' Election.    Tuesday, March 30th, 1926.

## THE CANDIDATES TO VOTE FOR.

### H. MERRITT.        A. WINTER.        H. M. SCHOFIELD.
### J. A. GRIFFITHS.  G. W. POST.  F. M. HAYLETT.  A. J. PEARSON.

Printed and Published by the Portsmouth Printers, Ltd., 38 Middle Street, Southsea. T.U.

*Mrs Haylett's Guardians' Election flyer, 30 March 1926. Barbara Davis.*

and Labour Party candidate in the Guardians' Elections in 1926, and as the Labour candidate for the St Mary Ward in the Municipal Election in 1929. She had been involved in the suffrage campaign and her family recalled stories of her campaigning on Fratton Bridge with a banner. The Women Citizens' Association was frustrated, however, by its failure to secure seats in local elections. According to their Sixteenth

*Mrs Haylett's Municipal Election flyer, 1 November 1929. Barbara Davis.*

Annual Report, for 1933–4, they acknowledged that it was very difficult to get elected without the backing of a political party so they offered each party personal and financial assistance for any woman candidate they put into the field. Unfortunately 'no woman was available to accept our help'.

They were more successful in securing female magistrates. Miss Kelly was the first appointed, in 1920, and another two were appointed in 1926: Mrs Minnie Malcolm and Mrs Margaret Palmer. By 1935 another five had been added: Mrs Elizabeth Long, Miss Bessie Reading, Mrs Haylett, Mrs Dora Thomas and Mrs Rosina Parker but, between them, they still constituted only eight of the total number of forty-nine Justices of the Peace that year. However, Mrs Jane Kingswell had been elected unanimously by her fellow-Guardians to be Chairman of the Board of Guardians in 1924. It was the only time a lady occupied this position. Miss Jessie Stephen had also stood – for Labour – in Portsmouth South in the December 1923 General Election. She contested the seat again in the next two General Elections, in 1924 and 1929, increasing her share of the vote on each occasion although the Conservative vote was split by an Independent Conservative in 1929. Portsmouth's first lady solicitor qualified in 1929 too. Miss Dora Wadeson passed the Law Society's Examination and was admitted in November.

Municipal matters occupied much of the business of the Women Citizens' Association during the inter-war years. It was reported in 1933 that they had devised a questionnaire which went to each of the twenty-seven candidates in the forthcoming municipal elections, seeking their views on four specific issues: the appointment of suitable women as Women Police Officers; the use of housing subsidies in the form of Children's Rent Rebates for poor families with children unable to pay current rents for municipal housing, and to secure the appointment of Women House Property Managers; the provision of a complete Maternity Service as recommended by the Ministry of Health, and the appointment of an adequate representation of women on all the committees and sub-committees of the council, either

# A HANDBOOK FOR
# HISTORY TEACHERS

EDITED BY

## D. DYMOND, M.A.

LECTURER AT GOLDSMITHS' COLLEGE, UNIVERSITY OF LONDON

METHUEN & CO. LTD.

36 ESSEX STREET W.C.

LONDON

*Title page of* A Handbook for History Teachers. *Edited by D. Dymond, 1929. Author's Collection.*

Dorothy Dymond, 1932

*Miss Dymond in 1932 when she was appointed Principal of Portsmouth*
*Teacher Training College. Author's Collection.*

as elected or co-opted members. They received only ten replies but all were in favour of the proposals.

Miss Dorothy Dymond is listed as one of the subscribers to the Portsmouth Women Citizens' Association in 1933. She was the newly-appointed Principal of the Teacher's Training College. She was no stranger to Portsmouth. She had been a pupil at Portsmouth High School between the ages of 11 and 15 while her father, a Methodist minister, repeatedly on circuit, was locally based as Superintendent of the Southsea Circuit. She won an Exhibition to read History at Oxford – and would have received a First if she had been a man. She received a certificate instead. Thereafter she spent two years studying for an MA at King's College London and spent a short period teaching before she was appointed as a lecturer in History at Goldsmith's College, London at the age of 28 in 1919. There she published her pioneering *Handbook for History Teachers* and *Introduction to Medieval History.* Within two years of her arrival in Portsmouth she would publish *Europe and England: Earliest Times to Renaissance.* She joined the Women Citizens' Association as soon as she settled in Portsmouth and had been here only a few months when she spoke at one of their meetings about the 'The Activities of the Civic Survey Club' which she had been instrumental in forming soon after she arrived. The aim of this body, she had said at the meeting held to launch the project,

> was to face two problems, a problem of education and a problem of society. The problem of education was to show the unity underlying various departments of knowledge and to keep academic knowledge in contact with daily life. The social problem was to explore means by which the individual citizen can serve his generation in these troubled times. One solution to both problems lies in a study of the City, in which all branches of knowledge are united. Everyone can make some contribution through his own observation and experience and social difficulties could be studied in concrete form.

Topics discussed over the next six years, all subjects of great interest to the Women Citizens' Association, included local industry, slums, housing and health. There was an exhibition planned for 1940 on 'A Green Belt for Portsmouth' but by then the club members had been dispersed by war. However, later politicians believe that Dorothy Dymond's influence then should not be underestimated and did inform official thinking. When the Civic Survey Club was set up, the times were indeed troubled. There was municipal progress in the 1920s and 1930s. Among a number of initiatives, slum clearance continued; infant mortality rates improved; a new Maternity Hospital opened, and a Child Welfare Centre; a new secondary school was built in North End; the Training College increased its number of places and a Municipal Airport opened. However, it was the dockyard discharges which began in 1919, and continued for much of this period, and the efforts to relieve the plight of the unemployed which dominated Portsmouth life in the two decades before war broke out again in 1939.

The Civic Survey Club's report on unemployment highlighted the fact that by the early 1930s a population of a quarter of a million had almost nine thousand out of work. Furthermore there were 3,500 school leavers each year, many of whom had great difficulty initially finding gainful employment. Some 19,000 local residents were in the Armed Services and another 13,000 were employed in the dockyard. Dorothy Dymond encouraged people to think about the need to create a better city with an improved economy which was less dependent on its traditional role as a dockyard and garrison – as the storm clouds gathered over Europe once more. Interestingly as early as May 1931 Admiral of the Fleet Sir Roger Keyes, the Commander-in-Chief, was railing against what he saw as the folly of disarmament.

War when it came brought devastation on a hitherto unimaginable scale. Nearly 1,000 people were killed in Portsmouth, not on a foreign battlefield but in the city itself, ordinary people, many in shelters in their own houses and back gardens, victims of the incendiaries and High Explosive bombs which rained down on the different communities from the first raid on 11 July 1940. Altogether there were sixty-seven raids. As well as those killed, almost 3,000 were injured. Nearly 7,000 houses were flattened, and over 75,000 houses damaged. Whole neighbourhoods were destroyed. Dolling's church, St Agatha's Landport, survived the conflagration, but the close-packed streets of adjoining houses did not. St John's Portsea was destroyed by fire and could not be saved despite the best efforts of the emergency services. The Guildhall itself went up in flames on the night of 10 January 1941 and was reduced to a burnt-out shell.

As they had only twenty-five years before, women volunteered immediately war was declared. A Great National Service Rally had in fact taken place on the evening of 27 April 1939. Over 20,000 people gathered in Guildhall Square that night and many more lined the streets through which they marched to the Guildhall from Alexandra Park, St Mary's Recreation Ground and Eastney Barracks. There were some 4,000 servicemen in the procession, Air Raid Precaution (ARP) personnel, nurses, ex-servicemen, Scouts and Guides, and hundreds of vehicles pledged for use to protect the city. The Lord Mayor took the salute and urged his listeners to persuade more people to volunteer. They needed several thousand more men and five or six hundred more women. One of the first initiatives launched once war was declared was proposed by Miss Kelly. Recalling no doubt the problems she herself had experienced in 1914, she presented a scheme to establish a Citizen's Aid Bureau to a meeting of Portsmouth Social Services' Emergency Council on 6 September 1939. It would in fact be the beginning of today's Citizen's Advice service. The original scheme, however, was devised at a meeting convened by the National Council for Social Service in 1938 as preparations began for the possibility of war and discussions took place on how best to utilise the resources of the volunteer sector whose energies would undoubtedly be needed when war was declared. In the first days of war, 200 bureaux opened across the country including Portsmouth's. Miss Kelly's meeting agreed that a Citizen's Aid Bureau was an excellent idea. Every public body would be asked to nominate a liaison officer who could be contacted by volunteers in the Bureau for advice on issues raised with them by the public. The first bureau was set up in the Girls' Southern Secondary School. Later, in October 1941, a Cosham Branch was opened. The volunteer workers, many in the uniform of the Women's Volunteer Service (WVS), dealt initially with hundreds of inquiries to do with the evacuation of schoolchildren. As the war progressed, issues raised included air raid damage, shelters, gas masks, rent, rates, tracing of missing servicemen or prisoners of war, pensions and other allowances.

The WVS was founded in 1938 as the Women's Voluntary Services for Air Raid Precautions to help recruit women into the ARP movement. They did indeed assist civilians during and in the aftermath of air raids. They also provided volunteers for the bureaux and played a key role helping with the evacuation and billeting of school children. It was calculated that by mid-1944 well over 2,500 women were not only working in the bureaux, but undertaking a huge range of additional work. A number of members belonged to the Housewives Section. Here they received training which included first-aid and firefighting, gas lectures and air raid precautions. Work parties undertook mending and knitting for the Forces. 'Make do and mend' classes taught women how to make their own clothes and cut down larger items of clothing for children's wear. There was also a children's clothing exchange scheme which they managed. Other schemes existed which disseminated information on how best to make the most of your food supplies, and how to carry out basic odd jobs in the home. They had volunteers in local canteens, and ran a car pool. Their younger members collected salvage and there was a Welfare Officer for girls enrolled in the Land Army. They were involved in National Savings campaigns and the distribution of supplies of orange juice and cod liver oil for children.

Miss Kelly also arranged for the recruiting and training of some 1,700 volunteers during the war to work in Emergency Rest Centres for those who had been bombed out of their homes and were homeless. She had six centres up and running by the time the first raids took place and at the height of the bombing there were twenty-two centres operating. It was hazardous work. Several centres were hit during raids. The bombed out victims came to the centres with only the clothes they stood up in. This was when the Lady Mayoress's Clothing Depot stepped in. By the end of 1943, the indefatigable Lady Daley and her team (her husband was knighted for services to Civil Defence in the Birthday Honours on 12 June 1941) had reclothed 32,651 people which had involved the distribution of 171,938 garments. It was a remarkable achievement. Equally remarkable was the achievement of Portsmouth's wartime Lord Mayor and Lady Mayoress in serving for five consecutive years. Sir Denis Daley was a former Royal Marine sergeant. He was elected to the city council for Kingston Ward in 1932 and was elected to serve as Lord Mayor in November 1939. He brought to the table a vital knowledge and understanding of what Portsmouth was all about. He was the man for the times and his colleagues acknowledged this in the faith they placed in him by electing him as their wartime Lord Mayor. His wife, Margaret, was younger than he was; she was pretty and energetic, and despite the fact that they had young children at home themselves, she threw herself into war work. Photographs survive of them both during the war years escorting their majesties, the king and queen, the prime minister and Mrs Churchill, and other visiting dignitaries through the devastated city streets, and entertaining them afterwards in the Municipal Offices, located then in requisitioned seaside hotels on Southsea sea front. They stood down in November 1944. 'Never in history had the task of Chief Citizen and his wife been so exacting', said *Records of the Corporation,*

> Five years of honest endeavour and great accomplishment came to a close with the prospects of victory and peace on the horizon, and with lighter hearts than those with which they had entered upon office in 1939, the Lord Mayor and the Lady Mayoress celebrated what was in the nature of a farewell week.

A farewell ball took place on South Parade Pier on 27 October 1944. All the Services were represented, and civilians included men and women from the ARP, the National Fire Service, the Police, and the Rescue and Demolition Squads, the staff of the local hospitals, members of the WVS and other welfare teams.

Portsmouth women were decorated for war service. Miss Kelly became a DBE Local hospital matrons, Miss Keen at the Royal and Miss Gay at Saint Mary's, were both awarded the OBE A number of young women were awarded the BEM for bravery and outstanding conduct during air raids. Dr Una Mulvany was awarded an MBE in recognition of her services in Civil Defence. She was the Medical Officer in charge of a first aid post in St George's Square, Portsea, and risked her own life again and again according to William Easthope, the Editor of *Smitten City: The Story of Portsmouth in the Air Raids 1940–1944* which was published by the *Evening News* in 1944. Once again, women had proved that they could do as good a job as men. However, Portsmouth itself had changed forever. Thousands had left the devastated city to fight, to escape the bombing or because they had been bombed out. Many never returned. The 7,000 properties destroyed represented a tenth of the city's housing stock. They included most of the property condemned before the war as unfit. Another tenth of the stock was severely damaged. Further, said Easthope, the principal shopping centres had been practically obliterated,

> there is not a part of the City which does not show hideous scars, in some places completely devastated areas. Our beautiful Guildhall has been burnt out and many of its treasures, such as paintings, lost, though the priceless Corporation plate was saved. Thirty churches and mission halls were destroyed or very badly damaged. Eight schools were destroyed, nine seriously damaged and 11 slightly damaged. One hospital was destroyed, another badly damaged. Licensed premises that have ceased to operate owing to destruction or damage number 150.

The problem of repair would be enormous, he said. There would have to be extensive rebuilding which could only be managed with government help for at present large parts of the town where people had lived and businesses had once flourished were now simply open spaces, cleared of the wreckage of the buildings which had stood there. Thousands of local people were living in overcrowded, wholly inadequate accommodation. The council had not been laggards in addressing the issue of re-planning Portsmouth. A structure plan was adopted in 1943. Satellite communities would be established on the mainland and the population density on Portsea Island reduced to improve living conditions generally and the quality of life, as the Civic Survey Club had discussed and urged only a few years before. Potential development sites were explored on the mainland. Some discussion took place on the possibility of acquiring land in Southwick from the Thistlethwayte family but in the end a substantial tract of land was purchased in 1944 just north of Havant. It was the Leigh Park Estate and of the 22,000 local authority homes built between 1945 and 1974, nearly half were built there. Within the city's own boundaries, land was purchased in Paulsgrove in 1945. Work must have begun almost at once for the first houses were completed by the end of 1946. The Paulsgrove Housing Estate was the largest post-war housing development in the city. It was designed on 'Garden City' principles with open space, back gardens and only short terraces. The houses themselves were well-designed, with hot water, bathrooms and inside lavatories. Some houses even had central heating. They were 'little palaces' and contrasted starkly with dilapidated pre-war accommodation in Portsea and Landport.

Dorothy Dymond was made a CBE in 1949 and retired in 1956. Determined that what had survived of Portsmouth's historic infrastructure should be preserved at all costs, most notably its fortifications, she took the chair of Portsmouth Museums Society in 1957 when there was a distinct risk that the fortifications at the harbour mouth would be demolished to make way for luxury housing. She described the society a few years later in 1965 as 'a unique institution', combining, a local history society with a civic society. It is interested in preserving the evidence of Portsmouth's rich history, and it is also interested in furthering the cultural development of Portsmouth today and tomorrow. In other words, we study the history of a community – its growth in the past and its development in the future – and we are concerned that this expansion should not only increase our numbers and wealth but also our arts, amenities and intellectual opportunities.

At a crowded public meeting called by the society to support the retention of the fortifications, she proposed,

that these buildings which meant so much in the history of the city should be acquired by the city, that these buildings which meant so much to the history of the nation, should still be protected by the city that had always safeguarded them.

There was only one dissension. The City Council took heed of the sentiments. Today Portsmouth's historic seafront is a key element in the City Council's marketing strategies. Dorothy Dymond and the Museum Society also campaigned for, and were successful in securing, the support of the City Council for the appointment of Portsmouth's first City Archivist in 1960; the administrative separation of museums and libraries and the appointment of the first city curator in 1967; a publishing programme which saw the launch of the *Portsmouth Papers Series,* also in 1967 (whose board Dorothy Dymond chaired); and, in 1971, the inauguration of the *Portsmouth Record Series.* They also played a part in securing a modern Central Library for Portsmouth in Guildhall Square which opened in 1976. In that same year Dorothy Dymond was made an honorary doctor of letters by the University of Southampton. The Public Orator said that 'Portsmouth's debt to her is beyond calculation'. On her ninetieth birthday, her Portsmouth friends presented her with *Hampshire Studies,* a *festschrift* of eleven original essays, in each of which an important local historical topic is discussed which has received little notice thus far.

The Portsmouth Women Citizens' Association was wound up in 1977. Would the members have been content with what had been achieved for their sex? At that time only one woman, Miss Phyllis Loe, the former Matron of St James's Hospital, had been elected Lord Mayor, in 1972. Another very senior nursing figure, Miss Wyn Sutcliffe, a former Matron of St Mary's Hospital, who had in fact served as Miss Loe's Mayoress during the latter's mayoralty, followed her as Lord Mayor in 1980. Over the next thirty years another eight women have served as Lord Mayor. Three women have stood successfully as parliamentary candidates: Sarah McCarthy-Fry for Labour in 2005, and Penny Mordaunt for the Conservatives in 2010, 2015 and 2017, both for Portsmouth North, and Flick Drummond in 2015 for Portsmouth South. Flick Drummond lost her seat in 2017, but for two years Portsmouth, the home of the Royal Navy, was represented at Westminster by two women, one of whom, Penny Mordaunt, was a naval reservist, and this at a time when more women – some 14 million – were in employment across the nation than ever before. Norah O'Shea, her fellow-suffragists and former members of the Women Citizens' Association would have rejoiced. They would also applaud the Portsmouth women who write about this city today. Betty Burton, Lilian Harry and Julia Bryant in particular have been inspired by much of what is discussed in this book: how women coped over the centuries in this 'most masculine' of communities, how they kept their families together against the odds, how they earned a living – and campaigned for the right to vote.

# End Notes

### ✳✳✳

There are no footnotes in this book. The lists set out below are a guide to the sources used which are discussed in the text. Material is listed in the order in which it was consulted and used. I do not cite sources twice in the same set of end notes

## Chapter 1

### Dockyard, Garrison and Naval Port

Masters, Betty, *The Growth of Portsmouth,* 1964. Rev. Yates, Nigel, 1979.

Webb, John; Quail, Sarah; Haskell, Patricia and Riley, Ray, *The Spirit of Portsmouth A History,* 1989.

Quail, Sarah, *The Origins of Portsmouth and the First Charter,* Portsmouth Paper (P.P.) No. 65.

Hoad, Margaret J., *Portsmouth as others have seen it (Part 1 1540–1790),* P.P. No. 15, 1972.

Hoad, Margaret J., *Portsmouth as others have seen it (Part 2 1790–1900),* P.P. No. 20, 1973.

Quail, Sarah, *Southsea Past,* 2000.

Besant, Walter and Rice, James, *By Celia's Arbour: A Tale of Portsmouth Town,* 1900.

Shuttleworth, Suzanne, *Farms and Market Gardens on Portsea Island 1770–1880,* P.P. No. 61, 1993.

Lloyd, David W., *Buildings of Portsmouth and its Environs,* 1974.

Riley, R.C., *The Growth of Southsea as a Naval satellite and Victorian Resort,* P.P. No. 16, 1972.

St Mary's Church, Portsea Parish Magazines, Portsmouth History Centre (PHC) CHU 3.

Quail, Sarah, *Portsmouth in the Great War,* 2014.

Wright, The Late Archdeacon, *The Story of the 'Domus Dei' of Portsmouth,* n.d.

Hanna, Katharine A. (ed.), 'Deeds from Portsmouth and its area before 1547', *Portsmouth Record Series* Vol. 11, 2008.

Quail, Sarah and Hardiman, Rosalinda, *Civic Plate and Sterling Silver: The Civic Plate & Insignia of the City of Portsmouth,* 1988.

Dymond, Dorothy, *Pepys in Portsmouth,* Portsmouth Museums Society Publication No. 8, 1977.

Jordan, Robert, *Portsmouth in the Glorious Revolution of 1688,* P.P. No. 54, 1988.

Field, John, 'Bourgeois Portsmouth: Social Relations in a Victorian Dockyard Town, 1815–75', University of Warwick Ph.D. thesis, 1979.

## Chapter 2

### 'Portsmouth Polls': Fact or Fiction?

Hoad, Margaret J., P.P. No. 20.

Hoad, Margaret J. and Temple Patterson, A., *Portsmouth and the Crimean War*, P.P. No. 19, 1973.

Field, John, *op. cit.*

Medical Officer of Health Reports (MoH) 1896–1934, PHC.

I am grateful to James Cramer who shared with me notes he compiled on slum ownership while collecting material for 'The Origins and Growth of the Town of Portsea to 1816', Portsmouth Polytechnic M.Phil. thesis, 1985.

Bound volume of Reports of Inspections of Slum Dwellings, late 1920s for Health and Housing Committee, PHC.

Sessions Calendars, 1842–1882 (4 vols.), PHC S7/1-4.

Dolling, Robert R., *Ten Years in a Portsmouth Slum,* 1896.

Gates, William G., (Gates) and successors (eds.), *Records of the Corporation, 1835–1974,* 7 vols. 1928–1983.

Diocesan Refuge Casebooks, 1886 – c.1914, PHC CHU 1.

*Kelly's Directories,* 1895 onwards.

Quail, Sarah, *Foul Deeds and Suspicious Deaths Around Portsmouth,* 2008.


## Chapter 3

### The 'Song of the Shirt': Trades and Occupations

Census Reports for Portsmouth, 1801–1950, PHC.

Austen, Jane, *Persuasion* (first published in 1818), The Crown Classic Library's *The Works of Jane Austen*, Spring Books, 1967.

Merewood, Thelma, 'Letters from a Portsea Parsonage, 1872–75', *Portsmouth Archives Review,* Volume 6, 1985 and PHC 879A.

Riley, R.C., *The Houses and Inhabitants of Thomas Ellis Owen's Southsea*, P.P. No. 32, 1980.

Diocesan Refuge Casebooks, 1886 – c.1914, PHC CHU 1.

Slight, H. and J., *Chronicles of Portsmouth, 1828.*

Gates, *Records of the Corporation, 1835–1927.*

Riley, R.C., *The Industries of Portsmouth in the Nineteenth Century,* P.P. No. 25.

Dolling, *op. cit.*

Riley, R.C., *Old Portsmouth: A Garrison Town in the Mid-nineteenth Century,* P.P. No.76.

*Hampshire Telegraph (H.T.),* 14 Jan. 1869.

*H.T.,* 19 Dec. 1913.

Records of Chilcot and Williams, Staymakers, 1849–1970, PHC 504A.

Lasseter, W. Lewis, *The Portsmouth Corset Industry: Its Origins and Growth.* Offprint of Port of Portsmouth Chamber of Commerce Journal, n.d., PHC 204A.

Lee, Sharon and Stedman, John (eds.), *Fingers to the bone: Recollections of corset workers in Portsmouth,* Portsmouth Museums and Records Service and others, 2002.


**Chapter 4**

**'Neat, trim and taut…'**

Hoad, Margaret J, P.P. No. 20.

Riley, R.C., P.P. No. 32.

Pevsner, *Hampshire,* Buildings of England.

Webb, *Spirit of Portsmouth.*

Francis, David, *Portsmouth Novelists,* P.P. No. 74.

Beeton, Mrs, *The Book of Household Management, n.d..* First published as a book in 1861.

Worton, Brenda, 'The Diary of Lady Georgiana Clarke-Jervoise 1863–1868', *Portsmouth Archives Review* Vol. 7, 1984.

Gates, *Records of the Corporation, 1835–1927.*

Yates, Nigel, *The Anglican Revival in Victorian Portsmouth,* P.P. No. 37, 1983.

31st Annual Report of The Portsmouth Rescue Society and Protestant Home for Fallen Women. Hyde Park Road, 1894. PHC.

White, The Rev'd Dr Sr Teresa Joan White, CSA, 'The Deaconess Community of St Andrew, 1861–2011', 2011.

Portsmouth Victoria Nursing Association Annual Reports, 1885–1909. PHC.

Peacock, Sarah, 'The Parliamentary Representation of Portsmouth 1885–1918, in Webb, John, Yates, Nigel and Peacock, Sarah (eds.), *Hampshire Studies,* 1981.

Washington, Edward S., 'Vicar Grant and his Successors 1868–1924' in Quail, Sarah and Wilkinson, Alan (eds.), *Forever Building: Essays to mark the completion of the Cathedral Church of St Thomas of Canterbury,* 1995.

The Reverend George Dawson (1821–76) in his inaugural address at the opening of the Birmingham Free Reference Library, 26 October 1866.

Welch, Edwin (ed.), 'Records of University Adult Education 1886–1939', *Portsmouth Record Series* Volume 5, 1985.

Webb, John, 'The City of Portsmouth College of Education 1907–1976', *The Portsmouth Grammar School Monograph Series* No. 23.

## Chapter 5

### Suffragists and Suffragettes

For a detailed account of this subject and details of the resources for study available, see Peacock, Sarah, *Votes for Women: The Women's Fight in Portsmouth,* P.P. No. 39, 1983.

The most useful sources of information are the back files of the local newspapers, all available on microfilm in the Portsmouth History Centre including the Liberal *Hampshire Telegraph* and the Conservative *Portsmouth Times,* also the Liberal *Evening News.*

Tomalin, Claire, *The Invisible Woman: The Story of Nelly Ternan and Charles Dickens,* 1990.

Katharine O'Shea (Mrs Charles Stewart Parnell), *Charles Stewart Parnell: His Love Story and Political Life,* (2 vols.), 1914.

Marlow, Joyce, *The Uncrowned Queen of Ireland,* 1975.

Portsmouth NUWSS Book Box, PHC 753A.

Harriet Blessley's Diary. PHC 1155A.

## Chapter 6

## War

For a detailed account of Portsmouth during the First World War, see Quail, Sarah, *Portsmouth in the Great War,* Pen and Sword Military, 2014.

Gates, *Records of the Corporation, 1835–1927.*

Gates, W.G. (ed.), *Portsmouth and the Great War,* 1919.

St Mary's Church, Portsea Parish Magazines, 1914–19, PHC CHU 3.

Report on War Work in Milton, *c.* 1920, PHC.

Records of the Milton Home Industry for War Widows, *c.* 1916-21, PHC 471A.

MoH Reports, 1914–19, PHC.

Local newspapers, as above, 1914–19.


## Chapter 7

## After the war – and unfinished business...

Records of the Portsmouth Women Citizens' Association, 1918–1977, PHC 167A/3-4 and PHC 1055A.

For biographical information on Dorothy Dymond, see 'Dorothy Dymond: Appreciations' in Webb, *Hampshire Studies.*

Barnett, G. E. and Blanchard, V., *Records of the Corporation, 1936–1945.*

For a detailed study of how people voted between 1885 and 1945, see Ashworth, Gregory, *Portsmouth's Political patterns 1885–1945,* PP. No. 24, 1976.

# Index

✳✳✳